Mapping the English left through film

Published by Folrose Press, London.
Paperback ISBN 978-0-906378-09-0
Digital ISBN 978-0-906378-10-6

Visit: fiimg.com/mapping-the-british-left-
through-film/

Mapping the English left through film

Twenty five uneasy pieces

Ian Parker

FOLR🌹SE
P R E S S

Folrose

CONTENTS

CONTENTS

CONTENTS

CONTENTS

*For Erica, who watched most of the films,
avoids the groups, and read
every d(r)aft piece*

INTRODUCTION

The FIIMG Mapping the English Left through Film project is but one way of describing how the favourite narratives of the left groups work separately and in relation to each other. The project picks up and develops a series of existing older commentaries on the nonsense that divides us. The left does not spring out of nowhere, but is embedded, whether it likes it or not, in a series of other powerful popular cultural narratives about power and resistance, and filmic representation is one of the most accessible of these popular cultural forms. Most of us escape from our dear comrades at one time or another and find refuge in film, and so it is all the more disturbing, perhaps, to find that films provide persuasive frames to illuminate what the left is up to as it tears itself apart instead of tearing down capitalism.

Tempting though they are, jokes about the People's Front of Judea are trite, partly because they have been repeated so often against the divided left

– a measure of incomprehension at what the political divisions are about – but also because the left itself already recognises the problem and enjoys those caricatures so much. It is often forgotten that most of the richest veins of humour concerning the fragmentation of the left, and their supposed humourless complaints about 'political correctness' actually have their roots in the left itself as reflexive self-critique. To make that critique constructively, we also need to know something about the shape of the problem on the ground. This is where this mapping through film project should help, so you know something of the terrain of the left in England.

The organisations covered in this guide are ordered roughly in order of size, but we know that this is, strictly speaking, an impossible exercise because left groups are notoriously cagey about their membership figures and prone to exaggeration about their influence. Like cult films, their weight in the left does not so much lie in how many audience members they have, nor what positions they hold in the social movements or trade unions or labour bureaucracy but in their perceived influence. So, the ordering here reflects a rough guess made from working through an equation that factors in claims for size, their impact on the political scene and, to be honest, where they appear on the radar in Manchester in the north of England, itself not a reliable guide since so much political work is centred on the capital, London, in the south.

Not only is this a geographically limited survey inflected by my own sectarian inclinations, limited to England, not including Scotland or Wales, and confined mainly to the Trotskyist tradition (or how organisations impact on or are impacted on by Trotskyists), but there is a limited time frame to the account. The time frame is set by the period during which the pieces were first written and revised, a period of radical leadership of the Labour Party, that is, between September 2015 and April 2020. This was a time of high hopes, for a left government with Jeremy Corbyn at the helm, someone who had his own history of engagement with the revolutionary left even though he was not a revolutionary.

Back to the Future

We begin with the Labour Party, a very large mass-membership socialist party, and trace our way down, second, through Momentum operating wholly inside the Labour Party. Although the time-period in which we freeze-frame each organisation is within that nearly five-years, the narrative must, of course, trace where each group has come from. The Labour Party is not only the largest but the oldest of the organisations, founded in 1900 and for many years part of the 'Second International' or 'Socialist International' (which still exists, bringing together social democratic parties from around the world).

Each of the groups has its own origin story and, in some cases, chosen trauma to mark its appearance in the world, its break from or expulsion by another group. History is crucial to each of these accounts, history which interweaves the fate of each of them; ties them together as much as it separates them from each other.

Once upon a time, the fourth organisation in this account, the Communist Party, would have been second in size and influence, after the Labour Party. The Communist Party, now a shadow of its former self after the fall of the Soviet bloc from which it was guided in its political manoeuvres, was once the British Section of the 'Third International' or 'Communist International' founded by the Bolsheviks after the Russian Revolution and then controlled and manipulated by Stalin. The degeneration of the Third International led to the formation, by Leon Trotsky and his followers, of the Fourth International, which operates as the compass for so many of the rest of the groups (with the exception of the Socialist Party of Great Britain which wanted nothing to do with the Russian Revolution and plods its own path, and Plan C which emerged from the more autonomist socialist groups operating in parallel to the Trotskyists). The Communist Party of Great Britain (Provisional Central Committee) is a mutation of an opposition group inside the old Communist Party, taking its name from the old CPGB, and from that old group comes the present day Communist Party of Britain, which has remained more faithful to its old Stalinist heritage.

It is from the Fourth International in its various incarnations that the rest of the groups emanate, and here we can identify three broad sub-traditions which depart from and sometimes reconnect with Trotskyism. The first sub-tradition is that of the second group discussed here, the Socialist Workers Party (the British group, not to be confused with the US-American organisation that was for many years the American section of the Fourth International). What became our London-based SWP broke from the Fourth International during the Korean War with its own distinctive analysis of the Soviet Union (and China) as 'state capitalist' rather than as a workers state (and so, logically, unlike Trotskyists, the SWP tradition would never support the workers states against capitalist states). And then, from that we have a constellation of groups that were purged or split from this SWP (or its previous incarnations), that include Counterfire, Spiked, Revolutionary Socialism in the 21st Century, Alliance for Workers Liberty, the Revolutionary Communist Group, Workers' Power and Socialist Fight.

The second sub-tradition comes from the fateful division of the Fourth International into two competing internationals from 1953 to 1963, and from one side of the split which called itself the International Committee of the Fourth International, ICFI, which was led in Britain by Gerry Healy and which eventually took form as the Workers Revolutionary Party. It is from that 'Healyite' sub-tradition that we have still with us the present-day Workers Revolutionary Party, a very different and reduced beast now, and the Socialist Equality Party, the International Socialist League and the barely-existent Spartacist League.

The third sub-tradition comes from the 'International Secretariat' of the Fourth International, the other side of the 1953-1963 division, and then the

'United Secretariat', USFI from 1963. (The reunification of the Fourth International was, of course, incomplete, with the Workers Revolutionary Party keeping its own ICFI going until it imploded.) It is from the USFI sub-tradition that we have emerging a third constellation of organisations that include Socialist Appeal, the Socialist Party, Socialist Action, the Communist League, and, of course, Socialist Resistance which is the present-day section of the USFI, and whereupon comes FIIMG, the Fourth International in Manchester allied with Socialist Resistance. Members of the three sub-traditions encounter each other from time to time in the Labour Party, Momentum and in Left Unity.

This is a niche project about warring niche organisations vehemently defending their turf against each other. There is something of Blue Velvet running through these accounts, and you might imagine yourself as Jeffrey Beaumont peering from inside the closet to see scenes of incomprehensible stupidity. In some cases there is misogyny too, some groups behaving worse than others, but in all cases you will notice that it is men who are usually in command, and men who, with power, tempted to abuse it. There are few leading roles for women, and we will need a more powerful socialist feminist movement inside these organisations to match and extend the #MeToo movement in the film industry. This is where we are now. These are twenty five uneasy pieces.

1

THE LABOUR PARTY

Total Recall from 1990 starred Arnold Schwarzenegger as Douglas Quaid, a 'lowly construction worker' who goes to Rekall Corporation in 2084 to have a brain implant to give him the memory of having been to Mars on a dream holiday, much cheaper than the real thing. He discovers that the memory is already there. The question that riddles the rest of the film is whether Quaid's anxious uncertain sense that his troubled dreams of being on Mars, and that led him to Rekall, were based in reality – whether he was always the leader of the resistance there as secret agent Carl Hauser – or whether this is a false memory that gives him the psychotic delusion that things are not as they seem, that he is more than he seems.

There are three key hinge moments that the

film, based on a short story 'We can remember it for you wholesale' by Philip K Dick, revolves around. The first moment is when Quaid learns that he may really already be Hauser, a fantastic discovery that tears aside the veils of reality and reveals another reality behind it that structures what we think we know. This is the Philip K Dick moment par excellence; there is another reality – it is not that another world is possible; it already exists. Quaid is, and always was, a secret agent and leader of the Martian resistance.

The second moment, a key scene in the film that elaborates a motif in Dick's science fiction stories which is not actually present in the short story but true to the parallel reality themes throughout his work, is the moment of decision, of radical existential choice. This is the red pill moment (borrowed from the first Wachowskis' *Matrix* film), one where our hero is faced with a forking path between two realities, one of which will spell disaster for him and everyone around him. But which? Quaid is told by the doctor that the red pill is 'a symbol of your desire to return to reality', and that if he swallows it he will fall asleep in the dream of being a rebel leader and wake up as what he was before. This second key moment is marked by hesitation and anxiety, and it is the bead of sweat on the face of the doctor that cues Quaid into this anxiety in the other; he shoots the doctor and his fight in and for his new reality resumes.

The third key hinge moment in the film is actually at the end, an unusually indeterminate and pessimistic denouement for a box-office bestseller – *Total Recall* was made on one of the most expensive film budgets of the time – when Quaid is sucked out onto the Martian planet surface after a reactor explosion and starts to suffocate. Perhaps he has successfully activated the reactor as he planned, however, and perhaps this has released oxygen into the atmosphere, and perhaps he lives. The final scene of the film though does not make this clear, nothing is certain, and it is possible that Quaid's dream of a happy ending (like that in Terry Gilliam's *Brazil*) is nothing but a fantasy he conjures up to console himself as he chokes to death.

LP

The key question that haunted the Labour Party through to the General Election at the end of 2019 was whether Jeremy Corbyn's three-line whip for giving Theresa May the go-ahead to trigger Brexit Article 50 whenever she likes, and on the Tories own hard-Brexit terms, would be seen as his own 'red pill moment'. This whip decision in January 2017 was a defining moment, and underlay the final denouement of Corbyn. We already look back with some fond nostalgia at what 2015 gave us as the first key hinge moment for left politics and for Corbyn when he discovered that he was at leader of the Labour Party. But what then?

The British Labour Party grew to over half a million members after Corbyn was elected leader in 2015. This was an incredible turning point for a political party that had been founded in 1900, and had come to function as the British representative of social democracy, the British section of the Socialist International (the Second International which became a network of reformist and ruling parties trusted by capitalism to manage piecemeal changes that do not threaten big business or colonial power). The Labour Party first became a loyal governing party of the British State in 1924, and presided over a number of important progressive initiatives over the years when it took turns to rule, including the founding of the National Health Service, during which time its membership rose to over a million. This was before it folded under the pressure of capital and then enthusiastically, under Tony Blair, implemented neoliberal policies as the natural and most efficient heirs of Margaret Thatcher.

The election of Corbyn did not shift the whole of the Labour Party to the left, but rather opened up the gap between two parties; The Labour Party of the Members of Parliament and the apparatus linked to the bureaucratic leadership of the Trades Unions determined to prevent any shift to the left on the one hand, and the grassroots base of members of local Constituency Labour Parties and affiliated trades unionists who were dismayed at the abandonment of 'Clause 4' of the party in 1995 which, when adopted in 1918, had called for 'the common ownership of the means of production, distribution and exchange'. 2015 saw something of a time-shift, then, a dramatic victory for the left and a complete surprise for Corbyn, a hard-working and trustworthy Member of Parliament for Islington North since 1983, who had barely made it onto the leadership ballot.

This was like a dream come true for comrades in different campaigns who had seen Corbyn up to then as the patron saint of lost causes, and it was as if the Labour Party had now been shifted into some kind of parallel reality. Things were no longer as they had seemed. This is the moment, the first crucial moment, when this once lowly worker with the Amalgamated Engineering and Electrical Union and then National Union of Public Employees suddenly becomes Party Leader, as if it was always destined to be so.

It was as if Corbyn had bid to have the secret agent for the resistance fantasy implanted in his brain only to discover, like Quaid, that this historical memory was already there, that this revolution was something like what Walter Benjamin called 'a tiger's leap into the past', redeeming the radical history of the Labour Party for today, reactivating it, turning it once again into what it might have been, a vital force against capitalism.

It was, for some on the left, as if the Labour Party was now completely different from the rotting corpse it seemed to be, as if it was no longer an old social-democratic reformist party working with the establishment, but now with the resistance. Perhaps Corbyn was leading the resistance to austerity that would turn the tide against the Tories. At last, a popular trustworthy figure, charismatic in a strange anti-charismatic way – something that appealed to distrust of old political bureaucratic machine politics among new activists – was really willing to change the symbolic coordinates of the left.

Between 2015 and 2020 the Labour Party twisted and turned between two realities. In one, Corbyn was indeed a force for change, redeeming his reputation as honest parliamentary backbencher unconcerned with power, and speaking out for the National Health Service, for immigrant rights and a number of other radical causes. In the other, however, Corbyn surrounded himself with some dodgy Stalinist and bureaucratic party-political advisors close to the Communist Party of Britain, soft on the Assad regime in Syria, for example, and he tried to maintain party unity by fudging the debate over the renewal of the Trident nuclear missile system. Worse, Corbyn sided with the establishment in Westminster against Scotland, repeating his pledge to win back seats for a British Party run from London, for his dearly-loved Labour Party, from the Scottish National Party. Those who flooded into the Labour Party to back Corbyn, and even members of some of the little left groups who joined, were already asking themselves what is dream and what is reality.

Corbyn's red pill moment came in January 2017. The red pill was a symbol, of a return from the dream to brute reality, of falling in line with the 'will of the British people' that had been lied to and duped into voting by a very narrow majority on a low vote for Brexit. Corbyn had, quite understandably, been lukewarm about campaigning alongside the devious and divided Tories for the European Union in the June 2016 EU Referendum, but he was ever since egged on by crowds of little Englanders who have been willing to play the patriotic card, to pander to British nationalism in line with their own delusional fantasy that Brexit meant Lexit (a 'left' exit from the EU). Corbyn's decision to whip his MPs to vote for Brexit in parliament was a disastrous mistake, feeding the illusion that 'amendments' in parliament would have binding authority on Theresa May (the vote gave her personally the right to trigger Article 50) and then bizarrely proclaiming that the fight would begin after the vote had taken place.

Some desperately claimed that Corbyn's cunning plan opened the way to another vote after the Brexit negotiations were over, but then it was too late. They pretended that our hero had not yet swallowed the red pill, that there was still time to spit it out. Some hope; disappointed supporters who already avoided attending Labour Party meetings after signing up as members were already dribbling away. What mattered were not so much the secretive strategies but Corbyn's own role as symbol of the resistance, what this vote meant for the left. The Labour right-wingers who broke from the whip were then, by 2019, being cheered on by some of those who voted for Corbyn as leader, and even many members of Momentum voted for Keir Starmer in the 2020 leadership election. And so, in a bizarre twist of fate, Corbyn, never a Trotskyist, though accused often enough of being one, was replaced by Keir Starmer who was once a member of a quasi-Trotskyist network led by former secretary of the Fourth International Michel Pablo. Disillusion with the 'Corbyn revolution' was already corroding the resistance before the bitter defeat at the end of 2019 and the election of a new leader in 2020.

It is as if our hero turned out not be to be Carl Hauser, rebel leader, after all and perhaps not even Douglas Quaid, lowly construction worker. The worst scenario, and this is how it seemed to some of those gutted at his inept mistake in parliament, was that, after whipping his own Members of Parliament into giving support for a politically reactionary vote, Jeremy Corbyn whipped off his cuddly beard mask and we did indeed find Arnold Schwarzenegger underneath. It turned out that we were indeed taking a short cut to the third key hinge moment in this story when it would end badly for all of us, in the form of the 2019 election.

It was not merely that Corbyn returned to the back-benches and that the Labour Party became a traditional social-democratic party again, a return to business as usual, but that Brexit was triggered under the Tories under Boris Johnson in a nationalist frenzy. Now the British nation state can expel foreigners, crush the rebellious Scots, re-assert itself in the world, and we could all hurtle to nuclear war and choke to death from COVID-19, as if we were on Mars.

2

MOMENTUM

Antitrust from 2001 stars Tim Robbins as a seemingly good guy entrepreneur who turns out to be a control-freak corporate villain. Robbins plays Gary Winston, CEO of a software development corporation NURV (an acronym for 'Never Underestimate Radical Vision'). He offers Milo Hoffman, played by Ryan Phillippe, a great position in NURV to develop a new programme called Synapse, a global media distribution network, with complete creative freedom. It is clear who Robbins is channelling for the part. There is a nice moment when Milo asks Gary about some neat bit of tech equipment and comments that Bill Gates must have one of those; 'Bill who?' says Gary.

Milo moves with his girlfriend Alice to Portland to work on the project, but things quickly go sour after it turns out that the source code that Winston supplied Milo has been stolen from other indie programmers that NURV has rubbed out. The twists and turns in the thriller plot include revelations that Alice and another co-worker Lisa, who Milo allies with to figure out what is going on in the corporation, are in cahoots with NURV. Alice has been working with Gary Winston from the outset, and Lisa is also a double agent who turns Milo in to the corporation when he is getting close to the truth.

The film, which carried the tag-line 'Trust is not an option', pits the idealistic high-tech every-youth Milo – 'Human knowledge belongs to the world' is his driver – against the Gary Bill Gates character who is a complex typical corporate mixture of bad faith altruism and instrumental power-hound; 'Are we making chemical weapons, kiddie porn, are we strip-mining?', he complains at one point, 'No! Why are they after me?'

This is a pro open-source film, with the real good guys – that's what Milo stands for – drawn into a corporate world in which knowledge and organisational control go hand in hand. The film pitched itself as part an ethical collective alternative to instrumentalist politics and against the reduction of truth to pragmatics and competitive manoeuvres. In this sense the film is about the breaking of trust in new technological forms of networking and is 'anti-trust', against monopoly in the field of information and 'radical vision'. There is even a culture-nature sub-text, in which Milo is almost killed off in a seduction scene by Alice with a secret stash of sesame seeds that Milo is allergic to.

M

Mobilisation for Jeremy Corbyn through new tech social media networks quickly became one of the signature strategies of Momentum. Originally a network formed during the internal Labour Party campaign to get Jeremy elected leader in 2015, it then crystallised into an organisation under the control of Jon Lansman, a new bogyman for the right wing press. They should have admired him for his corporate tech-savvy manoeuvring. Lansman established Momentum as a private company. It flew, quickly drawing in thousands of members, and so Momentum expressed and channelled the hopes of a grassroots movement around Corbyn inside the Labour Party, and was even open in its early days to those outside the party too. Soon it began meeting and gathering together the range of activists who had been drawn in by what promised to be a new kind of politics, including many of those who had been involved in Left Unity outside the party. Meeting and gathering was good for Milo, but soon this would all change.

It was not so much that we were all Corbyn – the bar for that kind of direct identification with Saint Jeremy was set much too high – but that we could all be Milo, and maybe Ryan Phillippe will stand in for us supporters in the future biopic of the Corbyn movement. Lansman will be played by Tim Robbins. The Alice and Lisa characters, unfortunately but tellingly in a left-landscape still populated by ambitious young men who reduce women activists to bit parts, will give a sexist aspect to the story of the rise and fall of Momentum, they are reduced to the status of onlookers who are re-cruited and then ditched in the course of the inter-play between different forms of power.

Momentum was fantastically successful in the immediate aftermath of Corbyn's victory inside the Labour Party, peaking at a membership of 24,000, and drawing in many of the new activists that had been enthused by a radical alternative, a membership that way out-numbered the profusion of little sects that hoped to feed on Left Unity and then swarmed into Labour to recruit new members there. One problem Momentum had to confront was how to organise these new 'Corbynistas' without allowing them to be picked off and used by seasoned far-left organisers.

There were thus three forms of organisation at work in this process – big, middle-sized and little corporate entities, each with their own varieties of Bill Gates' smiley but wily leadership: first, the Labour Party as a massive bureaucratic apparatus and host organisation determined to strangle the Corbyn movement at birth; second, Momentum itself under the direct control of Lansman; and third, Momentum groups around the country who, in different measure depending on the location, attracted and then resisted the rise of little Bills.

Some of the local groups, the one in Manchester as a case in point, were seized by little Bills who were loyal to London. Some intensive mobilising around the 2016 AGM which played to a new cohort of middle-class members who were suspicious of organised politics and what they claimed were 'inward-looking' old Labour and Trotskyist politics led to a shock victory for the Lansman-loyal right wing of Manchester Momentum. Dishonest attacks on activists from the Trades Council, those who had made a valiant effort to keep Momentum locally to the left and out of the grips of Lansman, and even channelling of claims of antisemitism when the left dared to support Jackie Walker at the AGM, were all put in the mix. As a result, most of the left have abandoned this group, left them to it, while some key figures in Manchester Momentum have, to be fair, pitched in with new left initiatives.

Meanwhile, high-tech Jon has battened down the hatches on the mother-ship by using 'new technology' and 'new forms of organising' to suspend all the structures of Momentum and turn decision-making into 'consultation' exercises, one of the favourite ruses of corporate management. This is politics reduced to business, and then the business ethos takes over. Meetings now come a poor second – window dressing – to media distribution.

What is the real momentum of this organisation now? In some places this Momentum is all there is of the defeated Corbyn movement, and the left has to make the best of it, but they must beware; trust has given way to an atmosphere of antitrust. In some places now Momentum is still the name of the game for 'Corbynism', self-organised and independent of London (and Lansman), and effectively operating as local franchises that have spun out of control of the main organisation. In some places Momentum was wracked by internal conflicts, and by the emergence of 'Grassroots Momentum' onto which some of the tinier groups like Labour Briefing lashed themselves as it sinks into its own self-created sectarian swamp. This mini-momentum without a ruthless CEO – the only thing to recommend it over its parent company – was a feeding ground for the myriad of tiny Leninist groups for whom 'democratic centralism' operates as name for robotic and dishonest manipulation of any other bigger network they can get their hands on. It failed. 2020 saw a proliferation of other left interventions inside Momentum itself, including 'Forward Momentum' and 'Momentum Internationalists', hopeless take-over bids.

In many other places, fortunately, and this is the case in Manchester, new networks of the left, including from the Trades Council, have completely bypassed Momentum. Some of those involved in 'Withington Labour Left' (formerly, until 2020, 'Withington for Corbyn') and other parallel groups around Manchester still remember the founding meeting of Manchester Momentum where the chair referred to the group by mistake as 'Monument'; so, not a progressive force but an obstacle. Many activists stuck with it for a while, tried to make it work, and then sought out better company.

3

SOCIALIST
WORKERS PARTY

Falling Down spins out a desperate narrative of confusion and mania, one man's response to increasing alienation, an increasingly crazy and violent response that feeds on that alienation to compound the problem rather than finding a way through it. Michael Douglas excels in this film, which was released in 1993, playing Bill Foster, a defence engineer estranged from his wife (who has taken out a restraining order forbidding him contact with both her and their daughter) and cracking. This is a man who wants to be in control but who is losing it. There are two key moments in the film that crack open the fragile ideological carapace of Western patriarchal capitalist culture, revealing something of the hopeless pain for individuals at the heart of it, and showing how these individuals are incited to thrash out at those who should be their allies rather than against the wretched political-economic system that has driven them into this mess.

The first moment is the first crack, the first moment when Foster falls. He is in a long traffic jam on the highway, people are getting agitated, his car air-conditioning breaks down, and Foster loses it, abandons the car and spends much of the rest of the film taking out his anger on those who frustrate him. This is a man who is blocked from getting what he wants, and immediate goals are configured as things he must attain if he is not to be a failure. He is angry, understandably angry, but his energy is channelled in destructive and self-destructive ways rather than in a collective process through which he might learn from those around him who are also oppressed. He acts alone to solve the problem that he finds himself in, isolated from others, and that increases the problem. Foster trashes a Korean convenience store with a baseball bat after the owner refuses a request for change, and in a fast-food restaurant he shoots up a phone booth after being unable to get access to call his wife. Foster is by now caught up in racist assaults – congratulated by a white supremacist in a military surplus store – and this makes him all the more agitated.

The second moment cracks open this complicity with the violent events of the day, the escalation of a situation Foster was himself trying to escape. Before he is shot dead after pulling a water gun on a policeman, he stands – and at that moment he falls, repeats the process of moral failure, of falling down – and voices his rage and incomprehension that he is actually in some way responsible for the carnage. This is the moment when he bewails the inability of the others to understand what is happening to him, what, 'I'm the bad guy!' I help to protect America he tells the policeman, I did everything they told me to, they lied to me. It is surely the most stunning moment in the film, repeating in miniature the incomprehension of the United States as invader and cause of carnage around the world; it is merely protecting itself, its leaders say, amazed that anyone could see otherwise, bewailing this situation by asking, what, 'I'm the bad guy?'.

SWP

Falling Down stages a symptom of masculinity in crisis in conditions of alienation and the mistaken attempts to seal off the self as a solution to that crisis. It is a failure that is indicative of the lives of many men, and also of many organisations and even 'opposition' groups under capitalism, even of groups that aim to overthrow capitalism itself. This is the peculiar and sad symptomatic predicament of the Socialist Workers Party (SWP) in Britain in recent years, a group mired in complaints about sexual violence, and responding to those complaints with increased confusion, denial and attack on those who raise the question again.

The facts of the case are well-known (as a quick Google search for 'SWP Comrade Delta' will help remind us of) – accusation of rape against the SWP national secretary, investigation committee reporting to annual conference that the case is not proven, mass resignations – and the increasing isolation of the SWP is very understandable, oscillating between some shame on the part of some of its members who dared to challenge the party leadership over what happened (with many leaving and setting up shop elsewhere in new groups, like RS21, that treat feminism as a resource rather than an enemy) and defiant claims that what is past is past and that now it is time to move on. In some cases that demand that we move on has itself been accompanied by threats typical of an abuser who has been caught out; shut up, it is time to move on, or else.

What is at issue here is the longer history and mode of functioning of the SWP, a party that was founded in 1977 out of the International Socialists formed by Tony Cliff in 1962 out of the 1950 Socialist Review Group after their break from the Fourth International (over the question of the nature of the Soviet Union and consequent responses to the Korean War). One of the enduring characteristics of the so-called 'Cliffite' tradition which was carried forward into the stereotypically male leadership of the SWP (and also into some of the groups that it spawned in many purges and splits over the years) has been control, and the other is urgency, urgency bordering on mania. SWP leader Alex Callinicos, a new role for Michael Douglas after Tony Cliff, runs the International Socialist Tendency from London. Yes, they are good at organisation and speed of response, but ...

Anyone who has been in the SWP or subjected to their antics in the front-organisations they use to recruit members, ranging from the Anti Nazi League (a success) to Stand up to Racism (tinged with hypocrisy after the SWP support for Brexit) – sign a 'petition' on one of their stalls concerning any one of a number of current issues and you will find yourself on their recruitment mailing list – will know well that they are control freaks of the worst kind. The organisational rigidity of the party apparatus – prohibition of internal opposition tendencies outside of the short pre-conference discussion period, for example – is also evident in their pre-meeting caucusing and then intervention and elections for positions in front campaign leaderships. Those non-members who are willing to serve as padding to show that the front is 'open' quickly discover that they are just treated as useful idiots if they speak out against the prescribed direction of the campaign.

And anyone who has been in and around the SWP at campaign meetings and demonstrations that they don't directly control will know that, not only does every party member repeat what they have read that week in their newspaper, which is tedious enough, but the solution always amounts to 'building a massive movement' against x y or z, and increasing our activity. A situation that is a 'crisis' is always, you will hear members claim, turning into a 'disaster' (or vice-versa). There is manic optimism in practically every intervention, the idea that if only you do this or that (in line with SWP priorities) you must surely succeed.

The problem with mania is that it expresses a fragile and uncertain grasp on reality, so that when things shift from optimism to pessimism, there is a long way to fall, and the fall-out often has violent consequences for everyone around. The rape-case scandal is still not over, with mass resignations over sexual abuse in the party taking place seven years later, in April 2020.

The SWP response to the crisis over sexual violence in their organisation was to shut everyone else out and to try and deal with it themselves – big mistake – and then to blame anyone who pointed to their own complicity in the mess they had created for themselves. That's what they still say if they are confronted over their mistakes; what, 'I'm the bad guy?' They don't get it, that they are part of the problem, that they repeat and reinforce alienation and patriarchal domination in capitalist society and in so much of the far left.

4

COMMUNIST PARTY
OF BRITAIN

Emir Kusturica's 1995 very long film *Underground* might look to some like a searing critique of ethno-nationalism, but it actually replays and reinforces the very nationalist tropes it parodies. The biggest clue as to how we should read the film can be seen in the director's own political trajectory; when the film was released, Kusturica was known internationally as being of Bosnian Muslim background, but he quickly evolved into a self-declared Serbian patriot. He later began work on a Serb-nation theme park Drvengrad, a joint project with the ethno-fascists of Republica Srpska, stumping up over ten million Euros to fund it.

The mystery now is why Kusturica's post-Yugoslav tragic-comic revelries would ever have been seen as 'socialist'; he has traced his own journey from old Stalinist socialism in one country under Tito to something that is much closer to the red-brown plague politics of Vladimir Putin, now the model of choice for ex-leftist one-nation partygoers.

The subtitle of the film, by which it was known in much marketing was '*Once Upon a Time There was One Country*', which speaks to the desperate hope of a return to a united Socialist Federal Republic of Yugoslavia, perhaps, but is actually also a long lament for the impossibility of such a hope. And insofar as it yearns for the past, it is for a Yugoslavia dominated by Belgrade, as is clear from the decision by Serbian RTS television to show the original 5-hour version (which was cut for the cinema audience) as a five-part mini-series.

The film begins in 1941 in Belgrade, where two near-do-wells boast that they have enrolled one of their friends in the Communist Party, and the first part of the film takes us through underground resistance to the Germans during the war, including time suffered by the main character after being caught and tortured. Part two moves from World War to Cold War and confusion about whether our main man is still alive or dead, during which time he is commemorated with a statue erected for him. This confusion is compounded by time underground – this is one underground referred to in the title of the film – and our heroes journey above ground at one point into a film set, which leads them to believe that the war with the Germans is still raging. Part three takes us through the 1990s Yugoslav civil wars. In the final scene of *Underground*, the musical folk drift into the seas while a cynical narrator speaks to camera, telling us that once upon a time there was one country.

CPB

There are plenty of deaths, rumours of death, and bizarre revival of those who should have been corpses in this film, but none so bizarre as the organisational revival of British tankie-Stalinism in the form of the Communist Party of Britain (CPB). If Kusturica's fantasy-film pins its heavy-handed metaphorical narrative on the link between the lives of individual characters and the life of a nation – here the Serbian nation as the real core of old Yugoslavia – so the CPB makes a big deal of its role as the voice of the British people in a 'United Kingdom' floating free from the European mainland while actually functioning as a little-Englander outfit to which Scotland must remain attached in a subordinate position.

The Stalinists in the old communist party, the original 'Communist Party of Great Britain' made a big deal about their own unity, with a supposed absence of the kind of splits that beset the pesky trotskyites (while flirting with the idea that Britain should be 'Great' again, viewing their 'British Road to Socialism' not only as a template for non-revolutionary class-collaborationist politics in Britain but a model for their comrades in other parts of the world). What united them all the while until their demise under the guidance of the Euro-communist 'Democratic Left' which took hold of the levers of power in the party in 1991, was actually their loyalty not to Britain as a nation but to the Soviet Union. Shed-loads of their daily newspaper the *Morning Star* would be bought by the Soviets in return for buckets of cash. There was some rationale for this craven subordination to Moscow until 1989 and the disintegration of the bureaucracy there, for the CPGB was defending what they thought was socialism; it was important to line up with the socialist 'camp', and so 'campism' as an international political strategy, which then played into national politics, made perfect sense to them.

There had actually already been splits from the old CPGB, the exodus of members following the Soviet invasion of Hungary in 1956 (which boosted the ranks of the Trotskyists in Britain) being one instance. Disgust at the disloyal Eurocommunist loosening of ties with the Soviet Union led a small group of 'tankies' – Stalinists who resolutely supported every armed invasion by Moscow – whether it was East Germany in 1953, Hungary in 1956 or Czechoslovakia in 1968 – formed the nucleus of the Communist Party of Britain, CPB, as early as 1988. The problem was that 'campism' quickly – with the disintegration of the Soviet Union and the transformation of Russia into a fully-fledged capitalist state under Putin

– turned into the defence of one camp of imperialism against another, into what has been termed 'Zombie Stalinism'.

The CPB then succeeded in wresting control of the People's Press Printing Society through bureaucratic manoeuvres and mobilisation of new share-holders, and so now once again it has the *Morning Star* as its daily mouthpiece, also a mouthpiece for a motley crew of misguided fellow-travellers wishing for the old days and transphobes wishing for a time when men were men and women women. The crisis in the far-left since the 1980s – control-freakery at the head of many organisations, and desperation in the wake of neoliberal consumerist new mass media that they could not control – has also led some old activists to flock to the *Morning Star* and then into the CPB; hardened Trotskyist organisational skills plus bankrupt 'campist' politics is a recipe for disaster, nationalist red-brown disaster.

This politics is driven by campism and by a Putinite international networks of Stalinist organisations. Thus, we are told by the CPB and the *Morning Star* that Bashar al-Assad, the butcher of

Homs, is a peace-maker, and this because the Syrian Communist Party (Unified) has been rewarded with a seat in government for playing go-between between Moscow and Damascus. Regime after regime is cheered on, ranging from China (where the Hong Kong protesters are portrayed as dupes of the West) to Nicaragua (where the crackdown by a government dedicated to private property is defended on the grounds that some protesters are linked to imperialism). This campism finds its way down on the ground to backing for trades union bureaucrats who spend their organisational energies on protecting their own jobs.

It leads to the idea that little island Britain, by which they mean England steered from London, of course, should go it alone; they are for a 'united kingdom' against Scottish independence. Now we have the old 'British Road to Socialism' dusted off, with the 'socialism' bit airbrushed out and effectively replaced with Boris Johnson (or by Jeremy Corbyn playing the nationalist card, if his circle of tankie-advisors that assiduously shielded him from his old Trotskyist friends had had their way). Putin has been pushing for the break-up of the European

Union for many years, and in the CPB he has the perfect political tool here to support that aim; and the *Morning Star* does its bit, publishing articles by those who once proudly declared themselves to be for neither Washington but Moscow, calling for what is laughably called the 'LeFT case' (Leave, Fight Transform) in which international trade would, they promise, be with China and Russia.

These guys really are the bitter fruits of socialism in one country. As with the characters in *Underground*; they have forgotten nothing and learnt nothing, repeating old international alliances, their 'campism', while repeating the call for old national alliances that are designed to ensure that Britain remains a capitalist state, that never comes remotely close to the 'communism' they sing and dance about.

5

COUNTERFIRE

In *Seconds*, directed by John Frankenheimer in 1966, Rock Hudson plays Antiochus Wilson, enjoying a second life after plastic surgery. He was an ageing businessman Arthur Hamilton (played by John Randolph) whose attachment to his loved ones had loosened and whose life was a dreary failure. Arthur goes to a secret organisation, known only as the Company, and pays them to have him disappear from his first life and old identity, and be reborn a new man, as Rock, Rock Hudson, Rock as Antiochus.

Seconds, after *The Manchurian Candidate* and *Seven Days in May*, is the last in Frankenheimer's early sixties 'paranoia trilogy'. Antiochus has to resort to a number of tricks to get out of his old life, to distract attention from his getaway plan and to find his way to the Company, and this trickery is replicated in the making of the film. For one scene in Grand Central Station, for example, commuters were distracted by the director's stooges having sex on the stairs while Frankenheimer filmed the main action using a camera hidden in a suitcase.

The hideous twist in the narrative begins when poor Antiochus begins to feel nauseated by his new life, being resettled in a community of 're-borns' like him. Their hedonistic lifestyle is unsettling and he yearns for his old life, even going to the point of turning up at his wife's house. She doesn't recognise him, and it pains him that he has taken such a drastic step. He eventually goes back to the Company to tell them that this isn't the life he expected, he now wants a new one. Bad move.

The company agrees, but then we discover, as Antiochus struggles on an operating trolley, strapped down while wheeled to a horrible operation designed to disfigure him, that his body is to be used as alibi for another new Company client getting ready for their own plastic surgery. There is a gruesome cycle in this film, then, as the main character realises he cannot escape his previous life,

and is eventually returned to it, second-hand, at
last a real corpse.

C

It began so well at the beginning of the film when
Arthur first escaped the old routine, and, released
from the old constraints, was as a butterfly emerging from a cocoon, now one of the beautiful people. He was, in this respect, very much like John
Rees who, sick and tired of the control-freaks of his
once-beloved Socialist Workers Party (SWP), was
able to break free in 2010 and, from being known
as Tony Cliff's 'second', almost as shouty but not
as charismatic, he was able to blossom as head of
his own outfit which he called Counterfire. Better,
he was able to get out of his old life before the sexual violence scandal hit the SWP two years later. It
seemed like a smart move. John is our Rock.

His resignation letter pulled out 42 SWP members immediately, and then another 18, and then,
with Lindsey German, founding member and con-
venor of Stop the War Coalition, these splitters
who knew well the usual next step of ex-SWP ac-

tivists (having purged quite a few themselves in their time as members of the SWP Central Committee) were able to found their own counterfire to the SWP very quickly. They succeeded in getting over 1200 people to London for a 'Coalition of Resistance' founding conference later that same year, a less sectarian version of the SWP front which was cobbled together a year later under the typically disengenous name 'Unite the Resistance'.

The Coalition of Resistance conference included some moments of high drama that turned out to be neat distraction techniques. Some members of the audience gasped as SWP apparatchik Chris Bambery strode to the lectern to deliver a blistering attack on the Tories' austerity agenda, very noticeably strode past John Rees, very publicly ignoring his old party comrade. As some suspected though, this was a stage-managed snub, concealing the real action; that Chris was just about to break from the SWP too, and pull out key members of the SWP in Scotland to form the International Socialist Group. Once again, the SWP was doing what does best, haemorrhage its members into nothing – many ex-members are so demoralised they leave politics altogether – or seed new revolutionary organisations that then go on to populate the landscape of the far left in Britain. The tragedy is that many of these new revolutionary organisations have been so well-schooled in the manic top-down mode of operation of their progenitor that they can't shake it off.

For a moment, though, it really looked like Counterfire was going to do something different, abandoning a weekly newspaper and producing free flashy newssheets at demonstrations, and having an ostensibly looser organisation without an elected leadership, until it turned out that this lack of accountability was nothing much more than a convenient mechanism for John Rees and Lindsey German to keep control. What was different about Counterfire, it transpired, was largely as a result of it emerging, not from a left split from the SWP (as the name of their tendency 'Left Platform' inside that organisation would have it seem) but from the right. This then had a bearing on their strategy of accumulating new friends and being very careful not to criticise them, first in the Coalition of Resistance and then in the much more successful recent initiatives of their new front 'People's Assembly'.

The People's Assembly, which was launched in 2013, has been a terrific energising force against austerity, and has succeeded in doing what the SWP always did best; make alliances with left Trades Union bureaucrats keen for left cover, draw in celebrities attracted by sharp logos and eye-catching protests, and manage them all by focusing on the kind of fake 'united front' initiatives in which the lowest common denominator is not only the guiding spirit but the absolute agreed plat-form. Here Counterfire are true to their own tra-dition of political work, with an understanding of the 'united front' as being much the same as the old 'popular fronts' of the Stalinists. For them a 'united front' means humouring your allies rather than, as Lindsey German should well know, build-ing the kind of alliance in which you 'march sepa-rately strike together'.

There is a logic to this approach – it worked well for the SWP during the early years of the Anti-Nazi League – but this logic also leads to com-promises that can draw the organisation closer to those it is working with, too close, something the SWP would risk tactically but which its democratic centralism prevented from leading to full-blown collusion. Counterfire encourages participation by outsiders in People's Assembly meetings – other leftists involved sometimes have the illusion of influence while merely being good foot-soldiers – until those meetings actually suggest something that goes against the line.

It is in its other front organisations, like Stop the War, that the logic of 'building to the right' has blossomed, and this has led Lindsey German to reign in criticism of Russia's actions in Syria (more convenient for their alliances with old Stalinists of the Communist Party of Britain) and to fall in line with the little Englanders on the left with shameful support for leaving the EU (and note that it was old comrade Bambery that was wheeled in to make that argument on their website) as if that delusional 'Lexit' strategy was in some way necessarily 'anti-capitalist'.

And so, the new John Rees and his friends have reverted to type, perhaps nostalgic for the old days of leading a mass-membership revolutionary party;

he seems to have tired of the reborns around him and let them go; Neil Faulkner was one casualty of being told what to do. This has prompted some of those who left Counterfire to repeat history, hopefully this time to learn from it. It is not simply that Counterfire has made mistakes, it is that it replicates too well its own origins, finds them impossible to resist. The Rees and German outfit is rather like the SWP they thought they left behind them. They are Seconds, second-life versions of the old organisation they yearn for, and whose practices they replicate.

6

SOCIALIST APPEAL

Jumanji: Welcome to the Jungle with the tagline 'the game has changed, but the legend continues' is a 2017 remake by director Jake Kasdan of the classic 1995 film, itself an adaptation of '*Jumanji*', a 1981 children's book of the same name. The format of the game is still much the same as in the original, with an old dusty video taking the place of a tatty board game, and the four characters are launched into a jungle in which they must find the escape route back, the key that will unlock them from this new world (the film was shot in Hawaii). The twist this time is that when they plug in the video game and are sucked into the surreal jungle-scape they are also morphed into a set of four avatars that are very different from their home-world selves.

The high-school teen gang are transformed into bodies that they will have to escape when they escape the jungle – babe Bethany turns into a chubby bearded male scientist (Jack Black), left-field Martha is now the beauty in the pack (Karen Gillan), the football jock turns into a weedy guy (Kevin Hart), and geeky bright nerd Spence turns into Dwayne 'the Rock' Johnson. There is a baddy behind all of this, of course, an evil explorer who wants to control the 'Jaguar's eye' stone, a magic jewel that turns on its owner, Gollum ring-style, and possesses its possessor. (As in *The Lord of the Rings*, this is a good analogy for the way that commodities under capitalism turn their owners into things so that those who frantically try to grasp the commodity find their own lives weirdly controlled by the objects they try to accumulate.)

Before the team get hold of the Jaguar's eye and pop it in place exactly where it belongs, in an occult statue, and shout the talismanic key word to return home they must encounter all varieties of animatronic hazards – hippos and rhinos and so on – and in this they are guided by a fifth-player Alex Vreeke (Nick Jonas) who has been living trapped in the game from the last time round, twenty years ago, as an aviator-explorer Jefferson 'Seaplane' McDonough.

It is a five-player game, but it is Alex who has the edge, plenty of knowledge of how the thing works from the inside, and (spoiler alert) it is Alex who doesn't make it back when things click into place and they cry 'Jumanji'. The success of the team, however, has redeemed history. Our heroes discover when they get back home that Alex himself has been restored to where he was twenty years ago; it is as if, dead to the world, Alex was more than alive for them as Jefferson 'Seaplane' McDonough in the game itself.

SA-IMT

If you want a spirit guide from the past to help you work out all the right moves in the class struggle then you can't do better than join Socialist Appeal. In fact Socialist Appeal, the name of the group which produces a magazine of the same name, is guided by a dynamic duo, one of which is still very much alive in this world and the other of which is quite dead. The live one is multilingual Trotsky-ist Alan Woods who runs the International Marx-ist Tendency, IMT, as well as Socialist Appeal as its British franchise. The dead guy who lives on as an avatar of all that was and is and always will be correct about Marxist theory was and is and al-ways will be 'Ted Grant', a South African Trotsky-ist Isaac Blank (a good proportion of Britain's best Trotskyists came from South Africa).

Ted Grant once upon a time led the Militant Tendency, itself an avatar in the Labour Party of the old Revolutionary Socialist League that bur-rowed its way in back in 1964. But Ted left Mili-tant, or was expelled depending on whose account you believe, along with his mate Alan Woods in 1991 when a large majority of the organisation de-cided, in what was known as the 'Open Turn', to leave the Labour Party and set up what became the Socialist Party.

Alan and mentor Ted stubbornly carried on in-side the Labour Party, and Alan, at least (not Ted, who died in 2006), has been guiding his comrades in there ever since; all of them with the exception of their very successful student group that to all intents and purposes operates independently of the Labour Party as the Marxist Student Federation. That was Alan and Ted's excellent adventure. Alan and Ted are twin souls (a double-role in the future biopic for a much older Nick Jonas perhaps), and much of the Socialist Appeal bookstall fare consists of the writings of Ted Grant as theoretical and practical key to action. The students don't just dust off old videos of Ted Grant or race around in multiple personas in the student movement and (sometimes, as they get older) in Labour Party branch meetings, they are also hot on theory, but of a rather over-heated dried up kind.

What is distinctive about Marxist 'theory' in the International Marxist Tendency and so also in Socialist Appeal, however, is that it is a kind of Marxism that functions as an all-powerful because it is true kind of worldview against which everything else must be measured to see if it is correct or not. This is rather strange because the Marxist Student Federation which laps up theory relayed to them from Ted (via Alan Woods as his voice on earth) are a bright lively lot, great activists and internationalists, but it might explain why there is quite a fast turnover of membership, and not so many graduate from the student wing into full-blown Labour Party politics.

Readers of Mark Fisher's ground-breaking book *Capitalist Realism*, for example, are ticked off for enjoying a book that is, we are told, 'a poor imitation of Marx'. It is clear that what we need is a good imitation of Marx, the Ted talks version, for example, that will show us exactly what's what and what to do. This is the other aspect of 'theory' for Socialist Appeal, a timelessly true frame that, if is really correct, will magically unlock us from capitalism.

They act as if they are the only Marxists in the world who understand what Marxism really is, and with this all-seeing eye on the world lodged in the right place, all will be right. This is surely the exact opposite of what theory is for Marxists who attend to the dialectical practical interweaving of ideas as they become transformed in new contexts, in new conditions of capitalist accumulation and at the intersection with other forms of oppression. It is as if the most radical core of Socialist Appeal, its student activists, have been set off on a wild goose chase by their guide Alan Woods for the magical talismanic form of Marxist theory that will, when it is put to work, bring Ted Grant back to life again and release him and them and us all from the capitalist jungle.

7

LEFT UNITY

Looking for Eric, a Ken Loach film from 2009, sees Manchester postal worker Eric Bishop (played by ex-Fall bass guitar player and walking talking palindrome Steve Evets) at the end of his tether. He is messing up his job and his life, and it will be the collective mobilisation of his fellow postal workers that finally brings him back to reality.

There are two kinds of reality in this film. The first is a fuzzy cannabis-induced dream state, false solutions to his problems in which his work comrades mix some stupid therapeutic self-help encouragement for Eric with time chilling out on pot. It is then, from this safe space, that Eric first encounters his hero, one-time Manchester United philosophical poetic footballer Eric Cantona. Eric Cantona becomes a kind of super-charged ideal of

Eric Bishop, his spirit-guide mentor, and big foot-baller Eric gives little postal-worker Eric the advice and strength to trust himself and his mates.

Ken Loach uses a cinematic directorial device in the film that has characterised a number of his films, one in which he springs a surprise on the ac-tor to get a more authentic reaction, in this case on Steve Evets who never imagined that he would ac-tually meet big Eric. The turning point is in little Eric's bedroom when he appeals to a life-size poster asking big Eric for advice, turns around, and finds your man standing there in the room. Loach aims to dissolve boundaries between cinema and reality, for the actors and for viewers who he clearly hopes will also become actors on the stage of life.

The second reality is one that little real-world Eric is now ready to confront, the grim reality of harder drug-gangs, gun-violence and YouTube blackmail. Now he is ready, with the big halluci-natory Eric's advice, to take on the gang leader, and does this by mobilising his worker-comrades and other Manchester United supporters in 'Op-eration Cantona'; in a glorious collective rebellion, they all descend on the house of the gang leader wearing Eric Cantona face-masks, trash the place and make it clear that they won't take any more shit, forcing the baddies to pull the incriminating clips from social media.

Solidarity is the watchword of this film, and Eric Cantona, who approached Loach and part-funded the film, is but a mediating fiction, someone that will galvanise our postie Eric into action, to take control of his life again. It's a great political comedy through which Ken Loach makes use of the big screen to re-energise non-celebrities, making use of figures like Cantona to build something different from the base up. But the rebellion is still cinematic rather than realistic; staged and feel-good, it is unclear how this dream-mobilisation will play out after the fun is over, giving us an inspiring moral tale in which we don't know what will happen when big Eric leaves the field, no pointers to what to do next. Could the next step be to form a political party?

LU

We had to wait for Loach's 2013 The Spirit of '45

about the formation and erosion of the National Health Service to spark an alliance of left groups and individuals pissed off with mainstream politics to try to build something different. Loach's call for a new party to the left of the Labour Party led to the founding of Left Unity (LU) later that year after his call was signed by over 10,000 people. The Eric Cantona figure in the history of LU, and Cantona should be first-choice to play our hero in any future bio-pic, our hero who is, of course, Ken Loach. Ken was the inspiration and guide for LU, attending the founding conference and other key events, until, that is, the nucleus of a new party to the left of Labour started to appear in a most unexpected place, inside the Labour Party itself with the election of Jeremy Corbyn as leader in 2015. Then Ken had done his work for all the little Erics in LU, marched them up the hill and down again to leave them to it, up the creek without a paddle, without a strategy, the fun and the party all but over.

As a result, LU is now suspended somewhere between two dream-worlds, between the optimistic heights of its influence with over 2000 members in the two years between 2013 and 2015 and a harsher more disappointing time of plummeting membership as people drifted, along with Ken Loach himself, into the new Jeremy fan-club and old-style party-political bureaucratic hell. The first dream-world was bad enough, and in some LU branch meetings a good deal worse than staggering through a smoky weed-garden. Would-be 'policy-makers' seized control of different commissions in LU, spending months hammering out pie-in-the-sky proposals which would, everyone involved knew, never be put into practice. These folks jostled alongside individuals who had either been burnt once by the far-left and who, understandably, never really wanted to be in a left party ever again and hardened apparatchiks of some of the worst of the existing revolutionary organisations who piled in, either to raid LU for new members or to steer it to a full revolutionary programme (that is, theirs).

In the middle of all this for these two years, the hey-day of LU, were individuals who really did, in the words of the tag-line of the party, want to 'do politics differently', and that included feminist and anti-racist activists who also wanted this to be a different kind of space, safe to talk, to share ideas and organise without being shouted down. This argument for much-parodied therapeutic 'safe spaces' in LU became one of the bug-bears of the hard-faced old left, particularly the little robotic battalions of the sects who used their paper to name and shame anyone they disagreed with.

LU as a consequence became very unsafe for a lot of people, a bit like coming down after a bad trip. Social media spaces for LU rapidly degenerated from being opportunities for debate into arenas for recrimination and threat, lurching from one ridiculous topic to the next (with one notorious Facebook discussion thread devoted to whether we should have the right to masturbate at work). It looked like we would be dragged back into the first fuzzy reality when nothing really happened, waiting hopelessly for the call to action, for the breakthrough into the second reality of collective resistance.

Presiding uneasily over these different kinds of politico-head very keen to give stupid and misleading advice about the way forward were Andrew Burgin and Kate Hudson; now the captains of the ship trying to keep it afloat. Helping them in the first two years was Socialist Resistance (SR), a group reluctant to lead and spending most of its energies trying to stop LU going too far to the left, to keep it functioning as a very broad left alternative to Labour. This was a group that eventually jumped ship and many of its members found what they thought would be a safer home in the Labour Party, along with mentor spirit-guide Ken. So loyal were SR to Ken Loach that members of rival groups accused him of being a member of SR. He was not, and, if anything, was viewed by many in SR as being 'ultra-left'.

LU was waiting for 'Operation Ken', but Corbyn's election did for that hope, and so the dwindling party was left on the rocks, still 'Looking for Ken'. Perhaps he was no more than a dream, evoking no more than the 'spirit' of free health care and a welfare state, welfare that is efficiently being demolished. The brute reality is that the Labour Party apparatus seems unable or unwilling to build a campaign against austerity, hobbled by its loyalty to local Labour-led councils that are implementing the cuts, even when Corbyn himself built up the

Labour vote on a radical vote during the election campaign.

LU is still an alternative, the best alternative in complex times, but not what it was, and now struggling to find the plot, and will have to do it on its own, a diminished but necessary force outside the Labour Party, hoping that Corbyn's failure will now once again be their opportunity. The nasty surprise now is that, when members of Left Unity appeal to their posters of Ken Loach for advice on their bedroom walls today, they then turn around and they find that he is not there.

8

SPIKED

Tomorrowland aimed to surf a wave of 'positive thinking' when it was released in 2012, driving forward an upbeat Coke-style 'teach-the-world-to-sing' can-do refrain. The illusory victim-blaming sub-text to positive thinking is designed to separate out those who can succeed from the rest, the losers. It was no surprise that it was a Disney production – it is named after one of the rides at Disney's own theme parks – but neither was it surprising that it lost money at the box-office, mainly because the audience couldn't work out what was going on. Too dumb, perhaps, and all the worse for them. Tomorrowland pretends to be open and inclusive, but it's actually geared to an exclusive club.

George Clooney stars as the adult Frank, who, as a boy, had visited the 1964 New York World's

Fair and, through a chance encounter with a girl android, Athena, visited 'Tomorrowland'. This world to come is some kind of high-tech futuristic parallel world, the tomorrow that could be, one that is potentially present around those who touch a magical T-symbol badge, a magical badge destined for 'special' individuals to visit and make tomorrow happen. Adult Frank, a demoralised recluse after having been expelled from Tomorrowland by David Nix, an evil-doer who is intent on sabotaging this super shiny version of the future, is mobilised by teenager Casey. She gets her T-badge after repeatedly hacking into the NASA base at Cape Canaveral to try and prevent the decommissioning of the US space programme.

Casey, when reprimanded by her dad for struggling to keep this technological dream alive, throws back at him the story of the good positive wolf and the bad negative wolf. Which is the stronger? The moral is that the stronger of the two is the one you feed, and she matches Frank's new enthusiasm for the possibility that the technological Tomorrowland will happen – 'We are the future', he says – with a desire to feed the right wolf. She's had enough of being told how bad things are at school – nuclear war, climate change, social breakdown – and voices the key message of the film: 'I get how bad things are, but how can we fix it?' Evil David Nix has prevailed up to now because he has persuaded people that they can't make a difference and that things can't change for the better.

Politics as such is named as part of the problem. Frank and Casey succeed by the end of the film, opening up vistas of progress as T-symbol badges appear around the world for the gifted who will lead us into Tomorrowland. Tomorrowland tried and failed to key into pragmatic optimistic commonsense, to embed itself in one of the dominant forms of ideology under late capitalism, the idea that technology can triumph, that experts should lead, and that politicians get in the way.

S

This is exactly the ideological worldview that 'Spiked' aims at, adapts to and replicates. Spiked is a case study of what happens when a left-wing group is led by a sociologist who has taken his comrades through their own blinding moment of disillusionment to be reborn as libertarians scornful of the old left they successfully separated themselves from.

Spiked, which today carries the tagline 'Humanity is underrated' on its website, has its origins long ago as the Revolutionary Communist Tendency (RCT) and then Revolutionary Communist Party (RCP), emerging from a 1978 split from the Revolutionary Communist Group, itself a split from International Socialists, which was a previous incarnation of the Socialist Workers Party (SWP). Even then, RCT/RCP activists were more stylish than the rest of the left, often referred to as the SWP with hair-gel. The group re-launched itself as a magazine 'Living Marxism' in 1988, folding up in 2000 after being made bankrupt by a dispute over the existence of Serb concentration camps which they claimed were faked up.

By then, 'LM' (these initials only by now because the word 'Marxism' was becoming rather an embarrassment and the claim that Marxism was still 'Living' was rather rubbing in the wrong message) had outflanked the pessimistic diagnoses of the end of the old left project made by the disintegrating Communist Party in its '*Marxism Today*' series on postmodern 'New Times'. LM's 'Midnight in the Century', authored by professor of sociology Hungarian Frank Furedi, an unlikely role for George Clooney in a future biopic, argued in 1990 that the crisis was worse than we could have imagined, and that the crisis in the left was irremediable.

The RCT/RCP sent comrades onto graphic design courses, devoted itself to media interventions ready for its reboot as *Living Marxism*, and eventually disconnected itself from the rest of the left, notoriously siding with the Union of Democratic Mineworkers during the 1984-1985 miners strike, and bit by bit took up a specialist niche position as contrarian anti-left commentators. Siding with the Serbs during the civil war and disintegration of Yugoslavia was one first step, and the next steps included hailing the possibilities of nuclear power and, since its rebirth as Spiked (and a host of front organisations such as the annual Battle of Ideas) pouring scorn on protests against the invasion of Iraq, linking with climate-change deniers and siding with Israel during the attack on Gaza.

This drift to the right has enabled and been fuelled by a concern with social diagnoses from outside the Marxist tradition – set reading at the still-functioning internal organisation meetings are typically classical sociological texts set by Frank – and this has also made conversation with 'policy-makers' easier. To engage in sociological babble about the 'elite' chimes better with policy wonks than old talk about social class.

Hapless sellers of Living Marxism during the late 1990s were already finding it difficult to justify their presence outside left events, claiming that they wanted nothing more than to promote 'debate', and now this 'debate' apparatus is in full bloom, ranging from the Battle of Ideas to the 'Debating Matters' events in schools and prisons. For some obsessive critics they are everywhere, with their tentacles through the media, and they love this exaggerated importance given to them, feed off it.

The rationale for the turn to 'debate' is precisely to side-step traditional 'politics', especially left politics, and to draw libertarian politicians and intellectuals ranging from Nigel Farage to Roger Scruton away from politics as such into 'debate', to enable a new generation of gifted leaders to emerge who will lead us into Tomorrowland. Spiked has spawned a new generation of younger activists who were well-suited to the new ideological climate, sons and daughters of old LMers are leading campaigns to trigger Brexit Article 50, for example. This then led the group to do a deal with Nigel Farage's Brexit Party, a lash-up which gave them access to EU and then British parliamentary seats, after which they were quickly out-flanked by the Tories who moved to deliver everything Farage had promised.

This strategy means cheering on the destruction of the welfare state – the 'Nanny State' that tells us not to smoke and how to think – and opposing censorship of all kinds as being the work of the thought police in the media and on the campuses. Frank inveighs against 'dumbing down' of education and against victim culture – a mantra that neatly links Spiked to the concerns of the alt-right – and his followers search out all manner of ways in which we are told how vulnerable we are rather than how inventive we could be. The twist is that this involves a turn to the right, to a concern with order rather than change; Frank Furedi's 2020 book on 'borders' includes praise for national boundaries, for the Orbán regime in Hungary, and for biological boundaries between the sexes, a favourite transphobe motif of late.

There is some truth in their warnings about 'victim culture', of course, but for all of the complaints about the 'liberal elite' telling us how to behave and think, this is a message for the elite: forget the gloomy predictions made by the old left, the question for Spiked is how we can fix things. The possible technological future is within our grasp, if only we would change our negative mind-set and dedicate ourselves to making it happen. Don't buy it. To be frank, this boils down to nothing more than thinking positively about 'debate', subscribing to Spiked, and hoping that being awarded a T-symbol badge will enable you to touch tomorrow now.

9

REVOLUTIONARY SOCIALISM IN THE 21ST CENTURY

The Wife, the 2017 film starring Glenn Close as Joan Castleman, real author of her husband's prize-winning novels, blows the lid on the crucial role of social reproduction, women's labour in every creative human activity. The film script and the novel on which it was based were both written by women. Yes, ok, it was directed by Björn Runge and also starred Jonathan Pryce as the husband Joseph Castleman who is invited to Stockholm to accept the Nobel Prize for literature, and Christian Slater plays a sleazy journalist poking around in the story and intent to paint Joan as victim rather than heroine. You always need these kinds of men, it seems, to drive the feminist plot on the big screen, but here it works well.

Glenn Close is the real star, the emotional pivot of the film, with a performance all the more powerful because she transforms her sinister-powerful persona, crafted for her by Hollywood in productions like *Fatal Attraction* and then hammed up in *101 Dalmations*. She has seized the typecasting of her as deadly woman – Alex Forrest stalking the poor married guy who slept with her, for instance – and turned it around, using it to give to Joan Castleman a cool studied power that will dare to speak truth to power, not in the spirit of revenge but in the spirit of dignified responsible action; what is feminism but that?

Joan has good reason for revenge, and as we track in flashback through her history as brilliant student at college – one who clearly has the ability to write – we ask ourselves how she could have agreed to sleep with her already-married professor Joseph Castleman and accept that pact to turn herself from Archer to Castleman, then to save her husband Joseph from the indignity of not being able to write, and to hide in the shadows while he took the glory. It was certainly a puzzle for the kids, wondering why their mother was locked away in that study all the time. This is, as one reviewer put it, Stockholm syndrome with a twist. She takes hold of the means of production, and by the end of the film we know not only that she will tell all but that she will speak and write, as she always could, to do that.

RS21

It took a long painful struggle inside the organisation before the last large tranche of leading activists decided that enough was enough and that the 2013 rape crisis inside the Socialist Workers Party (SWP), and the failure of the organisation to take the question seriously, meant they had to break from it. Some who had already left, and some who always knew that it would end in tears, thought they were too late.

The SWP had been spewing out new organisations in Britain over the years, as disaffection with the mainly male leadership and repeated purges of those who refused to comply took their toll. But this time it was different. Finally, a year later, after there had been a series of other resignations and the formation of younger groupings like the International Socialist Network (which itself split into fragments after a dispute about political correctness in representations of race-sex play in social media), the older battle-hardened seasoned socialist-feminists and their allies broke away to form 'Revolutionary Socialism in the 21st Century' (RS21).

Attempts by other groups on the left who had either been born from within the SWP tradition and flown the nest, or by rival organisations manytimes burnt by SWP fake 'unity' initiatives and front campaigns, circled around RS21 in 2014, waiting to pick up the pieces, offering talks about 'regroupment' of the left. And it is easy to see why. This was not one more mere internal opposition grouping that would burst into light only to fade away, fade out of politics altogether as many casualties of the SWP mania for total control did. This was the real thing, with comrades who had been accused of being 'feminist' – that was a term of abuse in the SWP who would weirdly pride themselves on their struggle for women's liberation – taking on that term and turning it around. The SWP under Tony Cliff who morphed into Alex Callinicos who was then morphing into Jonathan Pryce, were history, and pretty soon it became clear who had been doing the best theoretical work in the party.

It would be too easy – no, actually it would be difficult, that is the point – to point to one single figure in RS21 that Glenn Close could play in the biopic of the events in 2013-2014. It is true that there were plenty of scary strong women who went into action around the rape crisis; they had been scary enough over the years operating the machine-guns of the SWP in factional far left politics over the years – part of the apparatus – but now they were turning their fire back on the party that had effectively betrayed them.

In some respects, the new organisation also broke the mould of British far left politics, within a few years able to proclaim not only that a majority of their Central Committee were women – look at the history of the far left in Britain and you'll see what a big deal that is – but also to develop a theoretical underpinning for their revolutionary socialist group as one committed to revolutionary socialist feminism.

Partly through international alliances that had been forged over the years with other socialist feminist comrades who had also gone through the mill of the London-centric SWP apparatus, treated as appendages of male-centred 'Marxist' politics under Cliff and Callinicos, RS21 participated actively in debates over the nature of 'social reproduction'. First issues of their magazine embraced 'intersectionality' as a theoretical-practical approach to linking questions of class, gender, sexuality and 'race', and then 'social reproduction' became one of the buzz-phrases for a broad though theoretically-rigorous understanding of how it is that women's labour is central to the emergence and maintenance of capitalism; and, crucially, central to the emergence and maintenance of the liberation organisations that aimed to put an end to capitalism. RS21 thus give voice to the movement and manifesto *Feminism for the 99%*, and actively promoted the manifesto of that movement by Cinzia Arruzza, Tithi Bhattacharya and Nancy Fraser.

The emergence of RS21 was one of the best

things to happen on the far left in recent years, but we need to add a note of caution. Rather like cautious Joan Castleman, who is unwilling to take that last bold step to write herself into history, tell the truth and take up her vocation as novelist, until her husband actually dies (of a heart attack in the hotel in Stockholm), RS21 still often seem a little too closely tied to their old aging partner in the form of the SWP than is good for them. In trades union meetings, for example, we often notice the mainly women comrades from RS21 sitting apart from the mainly male comrades of the SWP, but still on the same page as them in many of the disputes with the bureaucracy.

They probably won't be completely free until the SWP is finally dead, and the process through which that will happen can only be a deeper more thorough-going revolutionary one that brings to the fore new forms of struggle fit for our times. The comrades from RS21 held back from 're-groupment' initiatives in 2014 because they were not ready to take that step, but one day they will take that step, when other activists have really taken on board the feminist politics they have put on the agenda.

10

SOCIALIST PARTY

The Remains of the Day released in 1993, directed by James Ivory and starring Anthony Hopkins and Emma Thompson, is a meandering wistful evocation of class relations of patronage, obedience and restrained resentment seen mainly through the eyes of Mr James Stevens (Hopkins) the butler at Darlington Hall. Set in the 1950s, the film follows Stevens after he receives a letter from a previous housekeeper at the Hall (Thompson), and borrows the new owner's Daimler to drive down to the West of England to meet his old colleague. The lines of the plot unravel through flashbacks as Stevens remembers his time as loyal servant at the Hall, which include the inter-war years when Lord Darlington dabbled in Nazism, an error of judgement which led to the eventual destruction of his former master's reputation and career.

The two threads of the film are packed with motifs of reminiscence on the one hand, as Stevens looks back at his life as a functionary in the great Hall, and decay on the other as we see England conjured into his memory at the very moment that it fades from old aristocratic power. The film, rather unsuccessfully, traces elements of the 1989 book by Kazuo Ishiguro who condenses a representation of peculiarly English class servitude into the figure of the butler, a figure who adapts himself to the whims of his masters and learns to bend to the rules while finding little spaces in which he can find some dignity while still being governed.

The book and the film are more about what has been and gone, the lines of regret and the comfort that comes from remembering the little gains that were made, than about what might be possible. Reminiscence in the film is as much about self-deception – the covering over of the moments in which Stevens collaborates with his employer when he agrees to dismiss some Jewish maidservants, for example – as it is about the attempt to come to terms with what has actually happened.

In this way the film is about being English and of Englishness as a condition for boring good behaviour, fitting in as the condition for being fitted up and so eventually being unable to resist. And so it is with the trap of reminiscing on the left.

SPEW

The Socialist Party of England and Wales members usually prefer the more respectable acronym SP – say it fast as 'espee' – to the more down-at-heel and rather unappealing 'SPEW'. They have a sorry history of oscillating between ostentatiously playing at being 'workers', proclaiming that their elected representatives take only the national living wage home with them (popping the rest of it into the party's coffers, then to be poured into the full-time apparatus and lost election deposit payments), and wanting to be taken seriously as having policies that will manage the economy well enough to keep Johnny foreigner out; free movement of capital is one thing, but when it comes to election or referendum time they effectively side with capital and complain about the 'free movement of labour'.

Their loyalty to the British state and willingness to pander to little-Englander politics flows directly from their many years embedded in one of the most efficient help-mates of imperialism, the social-democratic Labour Party. Once upon a time the British Section of the Fourth International (FI) as the Revolutionary Socialist League (RSL) dating from 1956, they began their journey into loneliness (and now they are well known for refusing to engage in solidarity campaigns they do not control) as 'entrists' in the Labour Party in 1964, putting into practice a policy flagged by their leader Ted Grant five years earlier.

They were so loyal to the Labour Party even then that they supported the expulsion of members of the Socialist Labour League (which went on to become the Workers Revolutionary Party) in 1959, something that soured its relations with the FI. During years of patient work in Labour Party ward meetings, they burrowed away into the host party flogging the very boring and distinctively shiny bright orange mast-headed *Militant* newspaper, and from then on they were known as the 'Millies'. That was until they came a cropper after fumbling their management of Liverpool City Council (where they controlled the local Labour Party) and then declaring that it was time to go in their 'Open Turn' of 1991, a turn from which they emerged blinking into the light as SPEW, spewed out.

They never recovered from the glory days of Liverpool, and it is true that the Militant Labour councillors put up a brave fight against government cuts, attempting to balance the budget and save services in the face of threats to prosecute them. And they never recovered from the very bad tactical mistake of dismissing council employees, shuttling around the city in taxis to deliver the bad news while promising reinstatement immediately afterwards. They played the game, and failed. What could they do? But instead of an honest balance-sheet of the successes and failures, they wallow in what they wish had been and deny any responsibility for their mistakes.

Ted Grant, unwillingly, it should be said, passed the baton to Peter Taaffe, landing a juicy future double-role for Anthony Hopkins. Taaffe now runs the SP, with Hannah Sell as deputy leader (our Emma Thompson), as well as its Trade Unionist and Socialist Coalition front-organisation from north London (the SP is last man standing in TUSC after the SWP decamped in 2017). And, predictably for a British group with any pretensions to equal status in the far left, the SP runs its own 'international', the Committee for a Workers' International which chips off sections every now and again from rival pretenders to the heritage of the Fourth International, and loses sections just as fast when comrades around the world realise that Taaffe much prefers the 'centralism' to the 'democratic' parts of a revolutionary party. Taaffe can sometimes suddenly turn into a grumpy old butler, and expelled most sections of the CWI in 2019, provoking a group in Britain allied with the majority to break away and form Socialist Alternative.

Those long years inside the Labour Party sure left their mark, and the 'Millies' could always be quickly detected by way of their habit of repeating the formula that an 'enabling act' would bypass the attempts of the capitalists to make the state work for them and so allow a Labour government elected on a 'bold socialist programme' to nationalise the top 200 or 250 or 400 monopolies (or whatever their favourite number was that month). There is that, and their habit of insisting that comrades read the *Financial Times* to discover what the capitalist class was thinking and so reel off lines of economic statistics, to mind-numbing effect in public meetings. Lower level members shook their hands up and down, chopping the air as they spoke in deadening monotone correcting each other about the latest financial data gleaned from the *FT*, middle cadre reached arm to waist with more velocity as they harangued a meeting, but it was Ted who provided the model, a living windmill who mesmerised annual conferences of Labour Party Young Socialists during the Millies' years of pretend power.

Other distinctive Millie political lines followed faithfully from their assigned role as a very English little party. On the question of Ireland, for example, they quickly adapted to the Labour Party view of the northern six counties of Ireland as being part of the UK, and argued for mobilisation of the loyalist working class as members of the British Labour Party (and, of course, if at all possible, as members of Militant and then SPEW). They also had a fond spot for the English nuclear family, perhaps another effect of remaining so long as butlers inside the great hall of social democracy, waiting for their chance to get into the master's bedroom and find the enabling act. And so they were very unimpressed with uppity groups like feminists or Lesbians and Gays Support the Miners, arguing that homosexuality was a symptom of decay. It was, at those moments, as if the good old red, white and blue-blooded aristocracy was better than pink degenerate capitalism.

Now SPEW, which had a central committee consisting entirely of full-time paid workers (until it ended the contracts without pay of those who went with the rival CWI which renamed itself International Socialist Alternative, ISA, in 2019), is really a party of butlers who are dependent on their masters for their living and so anxious to twist and turn to the latest line. Every British left group is afflicted with the pull of the past, repeating stories about the good old days, but SPEW is a special case. Please God that the British breakaway group Socialist Alternative, adherent of the ISA, does not simply follow in their footsteps.

Whenever we read copies of the outstandingly dull 'The Socialist' and the interminable references to the brave battle for Liverpool we are haunted by the dead-eyed face of Stevens the butler reminiscing about the past and going nowhere with it, apart from a futile nostalgic road-trip around old England.

11

PLAN C

The Dispossessed, first published in 1974 with the subtitle 'An Ambiguous Utopia' by feminist Taoist science-fiction writer Ursula K Le Guin should be a film, or perhaps not. Perhaps there is something necessarily ambiguous and so something all the more revolutionary about this account of a communist planet that is not pinned down, concretised in images of heroes and sanitised for commercial gain on the big screen. When it was published back in the 1970s the story of dissident scientist Shevek making the unprecedented journey from anarcha-communist Anarres to its capitalist twin planet Urras to work with colleagues he assumes to be freer resonated with the Cold War split between the 'free world' and the bureaucratic Stalinist dictatorships behind the Iron Curtain.

Le Guin's description of Anarres was actually explicitly based on the 'post-scarcity anarchism' of revolutionary US ecologist Murray Bookchin. Bookchin, who died in 2006, was once a member of the Fourth International, but gravitated toward anarchist politics with an ecological and feminist edge. But the problem, which *The Dispossessed* explores with a sensitivity to the lures of power, including to the 'tyranny of structurelessness' – the illusion of transparent debate which obscures still-potent hierarchies around dimensions of oppression and exploitation – is that Anarres was not at all a 'post-scarcity' planet. It was barely surviving in desert conditions of great scarcity, and so the pressure for corruption of power was all the greater. Anarres has been quarantined, cut off after its successful rebellion by its rich twin planet Urras.

Shevek discovers on Urras that a rebellion is brewing there, that the legacy of the revolution on Anarres is still alive, that the very existence of an alternative, for all of its limitations, energises a new generation of activists. And so Shevek is able to break out of the privileged academic-scientific elite bubble that welcomes and contains him as a celebrity dissident from another world, paraded as a symbol of rebellion against the supposed horrors of collectivism, and he connects with the resistance, realises there is more to the future than isolated individualism.

Another world is possible, but what 'utopia' is really, in practice, unambiguous? *The Dispossessed* traces the need for the struggle of the left within the left, of a continual opening of the revolution to multiple and intersecting forms of rebellion, the revolution in permanence. One of the great things about the absence of a film of *The Dispossessed* is that there is no one big star marked as the hero of the story, no one who would turn Shevek into a real superstar. He plays a key role in the book, but is more than anything a cipher for the differences between communism and capitalism and the struggle to ensure that the overthrow of capitalism really does arrive at a communist future instead of being stalled half-way.

PC

With most of the revolutionary left groups there

is a clear history that tracks the way they each try to replicate the struggle of Leon Trotsky, our 'old man' who resisted Stalin and tried to keep the hope of the October revolution alive and who paid with his life. So powerful is the sorry narrative of repetitive split and purge in the Trotskyist movement that there is palpable suspicion of new groups who seem to come out of nowhere, as if from dotted lines in the genealogy of the far left. When such libertarian alternatives on the edge of Trotskyism do emerge they are sometimes shunned, shunted off to the anarchist fringes (fringes as much fraught with rivalry as among the Trots) or avidly courted, as was the case, for example, with Liverpool-based Big Flame, a group that burnt the Fourth International in Britain in the 1970s, that was not as open to regroupment or 'socialist unity' as it seemed.

Remember that every real revival of a section of the Fourth International has come from new forces that are able to re-energise it and take it in unexpected directions; such was the case, for example, with the rebellions in the student movement in France that led to emergence of the Ligue communiste révolutionnaire which became a centre of gravity of the International in the 1970s. Perhaps the time has come for Plan C, a vibrant young or-ganisation to play that role today, and perhaps the existing affiliate of the Fourth International, SR, should join Plan C, which will then become the British Section of something quite different.

Plan C emerged from a meeting of 'Network X' in Manchester less than a decade ago, and linked together activists close to the 'autonomist' tradi-tion in different cities, significantly cities outside London, away from the traditional centres of state power and power of the centralised left. One of their few points of reference, not as origin-point but as source of lessons about autonomist politics recently has been the old Big Flame. So, the 'C' clearly doesn't stand for 'centralism', but perhaps for 'communes' or 'communism' (which is how members and supporters and friends of Plan C usually understand it). They are one of the nicest groups on the far left today, but niceties aside, what are they up to and how do they actually work with the dispossessed?

One of the key axes of their intervention has been in solidarity campaigning for Rojava, the rad-

ical experiment in Kurdish north Syria, an experiment of direct rule in which women have been a
visible force both in the 'peshmerga' resistance to
Islamic State and to the Turkish State in the local council assemblies. The experiment in Rojava
is explicitly indebted to the writings of Murray
Bookchin, and so we have an actually-existing reproduction of the Planet Anarres described in *The
Dispossessed*, an actually-existing reproduction in
exactly the self-same desertified conditions of isolation and quarantine, but with the added threat of
continual armed attack from fascists on all sides.

It is site of contradictions that betoken exactly
the kind of corruption of power that Le Guin de-
scribes, this is a revolution still led by Abdullah
Öcalan from his Turkish prison cell. Öcalan discovered Bookchin's writings, and wrote to
Bookchin, too late for that old ex-Trotskyist anarchist to be of help, and built those ideas into what
Öcalan calls 'democratic confederalism'. Women
are powerful in Rojava, for example, and they still
pose for revolutionary publicity in front of posters
of their leader Abdullah Öcalan. And Plan C too,
the good autonomists, are actually in practice a lit-

tle more closed and centralist than they seem, a perfect mirror for the Rojava revolution they celebrate.

Plan C also jump into line when a new leader appears, even if it is a leader of an apparently more cosy and comfy jumper kind at the head of the British Labour Party. They are good at organising corporate style away-days, feel-good festival style meet-ups with plenty of vegetarian food, but they have not been so good at arriving at a democratically arrived at decision about how and why to go into the Labour Party. Instead, members of Plan C, and not all of them, have dribbled into the big Party, led by example, led by their leaders, the ones who are never named as such, those directing a structure that pretends to be structureless.

The 'debate' about Corbyn and his legacy happened after the policy as such it is has been arrived at. They have been called out on this by their anarchist friends who are keen to make a raid, a version of the old 'unity' offensives the Trots practised on each other in the old days. This is not a film, and this is not an old Trotskyist group, and that is one of Plan C's strengths, something that could one day re-energise Trotskyism itself.

There is a real danger, though, that they will be eaten up by the fake-super-transparent-democratic autonomists rather than the Trotskyist left that has been genuinely trying to make sense of how politics must change in order to include all of the exploited and oppressed. They straddle two worlds, of the old and new left, ambiguous about what the plan is, about what comes next.

12

ALLIANCE FOR
WORKERS' LIBERTY

A Canterbury Tale, a Powell and Pressburger classic from 1944, stars Eric Portman as Thomas Colpeper, a magistrate and gentleman farmer who gives improving cultural lectures to the community, but who is then revealed to be the 'glue man'. This is the glue man who has been pouring sticky stuff into the hair of girls too friendly with the American GIs stationed in the fictitious little town of Chillingbourne near Canterbury in Kent. Colpeper's rationale for doing this, he says when he is uncovered, is that this will frighten the girls away from fraternising with the outsiders and so glue together the community.

In this film Colpeper is, in some sense, the obscene underside of the law, the smear on the community necessary to hold the good moral law in place. In spite of itself, the film reveals something of the dirty often secret violence that holds a clean wholesome community in place, a united community that in this film is configured as a very English ethnic community. John Sweet is Bob, an American army sergeant who gets off the train to Canterbury at Chillingbourne by mistake, and links up with Land Girl Alison (played by Sheila Sim) to track down the glue man after she is attacked on the first night.

A Canterbury Tale has become a cult favourite among a small group of devotees who visit Canterbury every year and declaim from the script, visiting Canterbury Cathedral at the end of their visit. They then re-enact the final scene in the Cathedral where the British Army Sergeant Peter (played by Dennis Price) plays the organ after deciding not to report Colpeper to the police. Bob has discovered that letters have indeed arrived to his sweetheart, and Alison has discovered that her boyfriend has not been killed in the war as she feared.

Just as Chaucer's pilgrims travelled to Canterbury, Colpeper says, 'to receive blessing, or to do penance', so Colpeper and his English community are blessed after having been glued together; the implication being that these desperate measures of deception were necessary after all, and the good that came from them will bear fruit.

AWL

The Alliance for Workers' Liberty (AWL) popped into the headlines in 2016 as the mainstream press tried to track down evil Trotskyists who were infiltrating the Labour Party, but their supposed crime of supporting Jeremy Corbyn and taking the Labour Party further to the left is nothing to some of the strange alliances they have made since they were formed. In fact, while they were busy circulating petitions against a 'witchhunt' in 2016, they were keen to reassure their hosts that they are very loyal to the party, taking the opportunity to draw a contrast between their own fealty to the party apparatus and the dastardly operations of nasty 'entrists' who are not really concerned with unity at all.

The AWL appear to operate as poachers turned gamekeepers, but things are more complicated than that; they are, at one moment, poachers who are willing to pretend to be with the gamekeepers, and, at the next, gamekeepers for the unity of a community who will do a little poaching on the side to glue things together.

The mastermind behind the AWL's twists and turns as they burrow into organisations and then emerge triumphant with a handful of new members out the other side is Sean Matgamna who founded Workers' Fight in 1967 after a brief faction fight inside the Revolutionary Socialist League (RSL), then British Section of the Fourth International, forerunners of the Militant Tendency and today's Socialist Party (SP). He then took the group into Tony Cliff's International Socialists (IS), forerunners of today's Socialist Workers Party, after IS made a unity call in 1968 and invited different organisations on the revolutionary left to come together under one umbrella (theirs). The story that went the rounds is that IS had their eyes on the International Marxist Group, a fairly important organisation at the time which counted Tariq Ali as a prominent member, but instead of Tariq Ali all they got was Sean Matgamna. IS paid dearly for their mistake, and Matgamna's Trotskyist Tendency was duly expelled from Cliff's group in 1971, though buoyed up with new members scooped out during the adventure.

Unity was now the name of the game for Matgamna, but unity with a twist, which was that each and every other Trotskyist group that made the mistake of responding to the siren calls of his group in good faith got badly bruised. Unity, it seems, could only be brought about by a healthy dose of internal strife. It set a pattern for a peculiar 'inoculation' model of entrism in which Matgamna's comrades join as very loyal members of the organisation they have targeted but then ally with part of the apparatus to attack enemies and so emerge as the winners at the end of the process.

Workers Power made the mistake of fusing with Workers' Fight to form the International Communist League (ICL) in 1975, for example, but things ended badly in less than a year. Matgamna shut down the ICL and its paper *Workers Action* in 1978 and launched *Socialist Organiser*, which styled itself as 'the paper of the Socialist Campaign for a Labour Victory'. Now inside the Labour Party, they managed to persuade Alan Thornett's Workers Socialist League (formed after the expulsion of Thornett and other comrades from the Workers Revolutionary Party in 1974) to agree to merge with them in 1981 and close down their own paper *Socialist Press*. It was another bad mistake, and the joint organisation lasted less than a year.

One of the crunch points in the faction fight that spat out the Thornett group again was the 1982 Falklands War and a response by Matgamna to the conflict which has been part of a pattern of adaptation to ethnic unity and notions of 'community' before the war and since. Before the Falklands War, Matgamna had already argued inside IS and after his expulsion, and against the anti-imperialist and Irish republication position of most of the British revolutionary left, that the Protestants of Ulster should be seen as a beleaguered community under threat with the right to 'self-determination'. It was an argument that was in tune with some of his old comrades in the RSL back in the mid-sixties (and there are traces of that in the Militant and SP positions on Ireland). True to form, Matgamna argued that the Malvinas were not Argentina's, but that the plucky Falklands Islanders did, just as Margaret Thatcher always claimed, have the right to self-determination.

The split with the Thornett group left Matgamna in charge to go on to found Alliance for Workers' Liberty in 1992 after *Socialist Organiser* had been banned by the Labour Party two years earlier. The AWL has been proving itself loyal to its host organisation ever since, and loyal to the different nationalist and ethnically-defined communities it has allied with. This is as well as having its newspaper operate as an outlet for Matgamna's poetry, improving cultural material that is clearly an embarrassment for the poor AWL members who have to sell the thing. Would that Eric Portman were alive today to play the part.

The adaptation to ethnic unity and community identity took another turn when the AWL followed through the logic of Matgamna's 1986 declaration that a 'two-state' solution was the only way forward for Israel, and for the defence of Israel. The AWL went on to forge a strong working relationship with Zionists in the Union of Jewish Students (more fool them, don't they know it will end in tears), leading Matgamna's bunch to argue that Israel is not an apartheid state, a position very convenient for its loyal membership of the historically pro-Zionist Labour Party. This is a position that has drawn the accusation that the AWL are 'revolutionary imperialists'.

Their particular alliance with Zionism also, rather predictably, led the AWL to publish Islamophobic trash, glue in the hair; an alliance, for unity and community, against outsiders. The AWL line, a weird perversion of the internationalist tradition they were born from, seems to be that community identity is an underlying good, and that a measure of deception and dirty work for the enemy will eventually result in something blessed for all.

13

SOCIALIST RESISTANCE

Groundhog Day, the 1993 romantic comedy directed by Harold Ramis and starring Bill Murray as weather reporter Phil Connors, was not an immediate hit at the box office. However, bit by bit it wormed its way into our affections, much as Phil did wooing Rita Hanson, played by Andie MacDowell. Phil discovered that he was stuck in a weird time loop with Rita in Punxsutawney in Pennsylvania, and had all kinds of opportunities for wooing her with different strategies that, he guessed, she would appreciate.

That's the joke, the hook in Groundhog Day; just as the Groundhog in the annual Punxsutawney festival revolves around a futile attempt by Punxsutawney Phil, the groundhog, to predict the weather, so our hero learns that he cannot get love by simply predicting and calculating what the other wants. Phil Connors repeatedly makes the same mistake, of using his knowledge of one day's events, one set of failed encounters with Rita, in order to impress her, to fit in with exactly what he has imagined she wants.

In the process of bettering himself, learning new skills to directly impress Rita the next day when the alarm clocks goes at 6.30am – 'I Got You Babe' blasts out every morning – he unintentionally turns into someone else, someone who actually is better; someone who was so dislikeable and manipulative becomes someone likeable and genuine. Phil has had to move beyond tailoring his every word to what he expects Rita will go for and, eventually, be himself. That's finally when he succeeds.

Punxsutawney is a real place and Groundhog Day is a real festival, but the film was not shot there because it is actually a bit of a dump (believe me, I've been there). There are two subtexts to the film, or rather to the conditions of its production. One is that Bill Murray was himself a bit of a mess at the time of filming, and was rather like the disagree-able character he played; he is a good actor, but you sense with Bill that he is always actually play-ing himself, something of the same grumpy grudg-ing guy he is comes through. The other subtext is that, like Lassie in all those old doggy films, Punx-sutawney Phil the groundhog is never the same lit-tle guy. A different groundhog is recruited each year to play the part of that furry Phil, and there are always a number of other substitute Phils on hand to step in should one of them not be up to throw the right shadow and whisper its meaning into the ear of the master of ceremonies.

SR

Groundhog Day might be touted as one of the most spiritually significant films of our age, but it runs on a premise unconsciously enacted by many left groups, and no more so than for Socialist Re-sistance, SR. Their wackier enemies on the left have a name for it, and are obsessed with it as the main obstacle to bringing down capitalism, 'Pablo-ism' named after a past leader of the Fourth International Michel Pablo. And because SR are the British Section of the Fourth International (FI) – the reunified world organisation that can trace its lineage back to the one founded by Trotsky and his followers back in 1938 – this Pabloism is all the more formidable a force on the practice of the left, not only in Britain. And, worse for the dedicated anti-Pabloites, as the current manifestation of the British Section of the FI – for many groups have stepped into the role over the years – SR comprises personnel from the old FI groups and some grizzled old activists who were themselves brought up to hate Pabloites.

In one of the more remarkable chapters of the history of Trotskyism, there was a significant merger of two groups – the Socialist Group and the International Group – in 1987 to form, wait for it, the International Socialist Group (ISG). It was the ISG which became British Section of the FI in 1995. That organisation went on to help found Socialist Resistance in 2002 (alongside the Socialist Solidarity Network and other assorted independent activists) and then took SR as a whole into the FI as British Section in 2009. That merger was so significant because the Socialist Group (SG) consisted of comrades led by Alan Thornett who were expelled by the fiercely 'anti-Pabloite' Workers Revolutionary Party in 1974; those expelled comrades formed the Workers Socialist League a year later before becoming, after some other failed encounters, the SG.

Meanwhile, the IG were seen as the worst of Pabloites, individual members of the FI, remnants of the old International Marxist Group (IMG), led by figures like Terry Conway. The IMG had joined the Labour Party in 1982, changed its name to the Socialist League, and then was taken in a weird direction under the name of its magazine Socialist Action advising key left Labour Party politicians like Ken Livingstone. A small group left to form the International Group (IG) in 1985, and they remained individual members of the FI. In Britain, then, there was a fairly successful healing of wounds brokered by Alan Thornett and Terry Conway, old enemies and now comrades, from the unconscionable separation of the FI from 1953 to 1963, something we could, for shorthand, refer to as the ten-year-Pablo-split.

The thing with Michel Pablo, and this, perhaps, is what makes SR what it is today, staggering on in its own peculiar version of Groundhog Day, is that, after the proposal to enter mass workers parties – the Stalinist International Communist Parties where they were big and the parties of the Second Socialist International (which in Britain is the Labour Party) where they were popular – came the temptation to tail behind existing movements and adapt to them in order to win friends and influence people. That's basically what Pabloism is, though in their defence, those accused of being 'Pabloite revisionists' and suchlike would say that we need to be where the action is, not just dust off Trotsky's Transitional Programme and hoist up the flag of the FI and expect people to rally to it. That's the way Alan Thornett tells it when he is rallying the troops, and so it is sometimes Alan who plays grumpy Phil Connors searching for socialism, and sometimes Terry who takes up that role.

Sometimes it really works, as in the turn to feminism, in which Terry Conway has been a key force in SR and in the FI; in this respect SR really becoming what they think they should be. In other cases it is difficult to bring all comrades on board, as in the case of Cuba where some cannot stomach cheer-leading the regime simply because other activists involved in Latin American solidarity movements tend to do that.

The recent turn to 'ecosocialism' that has been pushed by SR, and by its comrades on a world scale inside the FI, could be seen as the latest attempt to get their Rita, to win the socialist workers and make revolution. In the process, there have been some successes in building alliances, and SR have often endeared themselves by pouring their energies into joint projects that they were careful not to control. But then, there are moments when this goes wrong, when the Phil Connors leadership of SR go too far repeating back the message they think the others want to hear; a case in point is the embarrassing 'ecosocialist' defence of population control which Thornett will bang on about while other SR comrades look at their shoes and wish they could change the topic.

The comrades of SR have become who they are, really honestly authentically reconfiguring themselves to what they imagine and hope others will want, and want of them, but, this is the problem, still all the same mutating, chameleon-like to adjust their politics to each new political movement they hope to impress. The deepest underlying problem is that while they do have their eyes on a prize they can still just about name – revolutionary socialist transformation of capitalist society into a world in which we will treat each other as human beings instead of as objects - just as Phil Connors has his eyes on Rita Hanson in the film, SR twists and turns to give this future goal a different name each time it twists and turns to make itself loveable. This is, after all, of a piece with the FI itself, and it is not surprising, perhaps, that recent meetings of its own 'International Committee' of the reunified FI have embarked on a discussion of what socialism would actually look like. Meanwhile, as it burrowed into the Labour Party in its new guise as Corbynite, SR in Britain dropped the perhaps offensive term 'revolutionary' from the masthead of its website.

There is a happy end to Groundhog Day, but that is cinematic fantasy. Meantime, we are stuck in SR with the real world in which socialism is not yet on the horizon. They keep trying out new tricks, waiting for applause, and maybe, one day, they will hit the right note, build the kind of limited alliances they have been so good at forming in the past, and really be part of a revolutionary mass movement.

14

REVOLUTIONARY COMMUNIST GROUP

Zulu Dawn is a 1979 racist classic directed by Douglas Hickox, and starring a ripe old cast including Peter O'Toole as Lt. General Lord Chelmsford, commander of British forces. He aimed to take his troops into Zululand from Natal in South Africa in 1879, despite warnings from British and Boer military advisors that this would fail. Chelmsford tries to blame the predictable disastrous defeat at the hands of the Zulu army at the Battle of Isandlwana, the culmination of the film, on Colonel Anthony Durnford, Burt Lancaster. Burt Lancaster plays the reasonable more humane colonial ruler, with some kind of drifting location Irish accent, and is killed during the big battle, set against brutal Peter O'Toole who has been enjoying lunch during the massacre of the Brit forces at the hands of the Zulus, having dished out the dictum that guides him, that 'for the savage as for the child, chastisement is sometimes a blessing'.

The racist stereotypes that litter the film are lathered with liberal guilt over the studied and sometimes well-meaning incompetence of the colonialists, something that is supposed to justify the images of desperation and death. Other assorted character actors, such as Denholm Elliott as Colonel Henry Pulleine, are too decent by half, and when the good white guy is found writing a last letter to his wife back in Blighty he cannot bring himself to shoot his Zulu ex-prisoner, who then duly shoots Pulleine. Also perishing, to the angst of cinema audiences, no doubt, is John Mills as the British High Commissioner for South Africa, Sir Henry Bartle Frere.

This all sets the scene for the successful defence of Rorke's Drift by a small British contingent shortly afterwards, so fuelling a sense of high-minded defiance, resistance against the Zulus during that more iconic colonial moment. So they all fall, and the film itself, shot in South Africa with the assistance of the then apartheid Minister of Information Connie Mulder, operates as an exercise in bad faith, the Zulu extras being paid less than the dog. There are a few historical and technical quibbles about the film, but that's beside the point. Although the film did badly at the box office, its distributors soldiered on, and it eventually became a staple of afternoon television. Here are plucky Brits under siege, bravely carrying on against insuperable odds and advice from comrades and friends that it would end badly.

RCG

You need to track the way this film operates as an ideological document of colonial history in order to understand how it has hooked so many gung-ho supporters of British imperialism as well as hand-wringing liberals agonising about what is to be done about the natives when we have behaved badly and they behave badly in return. Instead of doing that, you can flip over a reading of the film, as if viewing the negative copy, and you'll then find quite a neat narrative about a tiny group that puts the fight against racism and imperialism at the centre of its work; the Revolutionary Communist Group, RCG, its troops commanded by David Yaffe. You won't find many groups more committed to a black and white reading of colonial history than the RCG, a reading which leads them to steadfastly avoid political alliances with anyone or everyone because every other political force is treated as a racist rival and obstacle.

It should be said that David Yaffe, a former Sussex University academic who specialised in the falling rate of profit – inventing a 'velocitometer' to measure it in detail – comes across as a nice guy; taking the trouble to humorously and rather self-deprecatingly inform readers of the Guardian in 1999 that his machine disintegrated in the 1987 stock-market crash. Peter O'Toole could play this little left-sect general in a future biopic of the RCG, which would admittedly be rather unfair. Read the trajectory of the group instead as besieged by the rest of the white left complicit in imperialism, as Zulu Dawn played out in negative, not positive direct form.

Yaffe had led a split from International Socialists, the previous incarnation of the Socialist Workers Party, in 1974, forming the Revolutionary Communist Group soon after (quickly dispatching his rival Frank Furedi (not Burt Lancaster) in a quick purge which led to the birth of the current that mutated into Spiked). But Yaffe can't blame Furedi, his Durnford compatriot for the disastrous politics he was himself about to enact with his always-beleaguered band.

The RCG are visible on demonstrations, and on their own street stalls as sellers of Fight Racism, Fight Imperialism (FRFI), by which they do their very best to alienate the rest of the left. RCG and FRFI shot to prominence through its non-stop picket of the South African embassy for ten years from 1982 through its own front organisation City of London Anti-Apartheid Group, pissing off the main Anti-Apartheid Movement by demanding the struggle against racism in South Africa be linked to the struggle against the British state (this at a time that the Anti-Apartheid Movement was doing its best to build the broadest possible Boycott, Sanctions and Divestment campaign).

They then turned their attention to the Palestine Solidarity Campaign, PSC, insisting on a perpetual picket of Marks and Spencer stores, starting in Manchester and then expanding to other stores in other parts of the country, this to the embarrassment of PSC activists who had been doing their best to distinguish anti-Zionism from anti-semitism. The RCG claimed to make the same distinction, but somehow their obsessive focus on the Jewish character of Marks and Spencer led them to unhelpfully muddle the issue again. At protests against Israeli apartheid in Manchester, for example, the RCG still try to divert marches to shout at Marks and Spencer while more sensible Palestine activists do their best to keep the march on track.

Things are always black and white for the RCG, and their support for Cuba, claiming that it is socialist, and that any criticism of that socialist anti-imperialist government is to play into the hands of imperialism, leads them to some strange and unpleasant manoeuvres. This is where Peter O'Toole as General Lord Chelmsford could himself be directing RCG operations, here as operations that seem designed to be 'anti-imperialist' but actually backfire. When Socialist Resistance – a group that can hardly be considered hostile to Cuba – organised a day-school in London in 2006, for example, the RCG did their level best to alert the Cuban government to block Celia Hart Santamaria from coming over to talk about her book *It's Never Too Late to Love or Rebel*, which was linking reflections on the Cuban revolution with Trotskyist perspectives on Stalinism.

The RCG is quick to draw round the wagons and treat every other member of every other group as a hostile force. They posture as the authentic only true voice of anti-imperialism, valiantly going into enemy territory to put up the flag, waiting to be shot down, almost as if that is what they always wanted. Their posturing and provocations at demonstrations puts the rest of the left at risk. They have consistently attacked the Labour Party in some weird counter-effective stunts, and then intervened to attack Left Unity on the basis that it was soft on Labour, this mainly because at one time Left Unity did threaten to actually bring the left together.

RCG stand at their bookstalls shooting suspicious looks at anyone they recognise, glaring at them if they come too close. Most everyone they know has already been encountered and denounced. It is as if they are getting ready for their own Rorke's Drift to show they were always right, but they actually set themselves up as the victims at repeated battles of Isandlwana, as if identifying with the victims of racism will absolve them from responsibility for the harm they are actually doing to the left.

They are, to put it simply, ultra-left saboteurs who have learnt from the very kind of Stalinism the IS/SWP tradition had tried to set itself against, and ended up mimicking Stalinist methods. They have isolated themselves in the process, despite the warnings of those around them who wanted to be their friends, and they will be isolated from any mass movement that actually brings about socialism in Britain.

15

WORKERS' POWER

The Wrong Trousers directed by Nick Park in 1993 was one of three very successful stop-motion animation films starring Wallace and Gromit, a toothy eccentric inventor voiced by Peter Sallis, and his dog. The film was made and released between *A Grand Day Out* (1989) and *A Close Shave* (1995), but should be seen as the third culminating episode in the career of this loveable clay-fiction master and his loyal though often exasperated best friend.

A Grand Day Out takes Wallace and Gromit to the moon, the logical place to go when they have run out of cheese. The rocket that takes them there is one of many weird contraptions dreamt up by our wacky inventor hero and off they go, where Wallace discovers that the moon tastes like Wensleydale – good – but that a local cooker-creature doesn't want them to take it. (Their love of Wensleydale, by the way, boosted British exports of this crumbly rather second-rate creamy stuff when Wallace and Gromit films became popular.)

Then, in *A Close Shave*, new characters come onto the scene – Wendolene, her dog Preston, and Shaun the sheep – and it takes a few twists and turns of the plot for Wallace and Gromit, separated in the shenanigans that ensue, to get back together again. No plot spoilers here, that would be too cruel. But our hearts are in our mouths as we watch strange possible new alliances form that might expand the Wallace and Gromit household. Sadly, those fruitful alliances seem, after the event, to have been doomed to failure.

In *The Wrong Trousers*, Wallace gives Gromit a pair of techno-trousers for his birthday, but ends up being trapped by them himself when the penguin he had taken in as a lodger gets hold of the control mechanism, and it takes sleeping Wallace off to the museum to steal a valuable diamond. It takes a while for poor Gromit, who has been sidelined by the penguin after winning Wallace's affection, to work out what has been going on, and longer for Gromit to find a way of warning Wallace and exposing the penguin's wicked scheme.

WP

Workers' Power's Grand Day Out was in 1974, when dissident members of the International Socialists (now SWP) puked up another internal group into the outside world that had been organising as the 'Left Faction'. They had run out of ideas in the SWP, so it was time to go and find some new ones outside. Luckily, or not, for the Trotskyists, this new group gravitated over the next five years or so away from the idea that Russia was 'state capitalist' (the calling card analysis of IS/SWP) toward the more standard Trotskyist position that it was a degenerate workers state. It clarified this position, as if it was a completely new home-grown invention, and in the process did battle with other unfortunate left groups which it merged with and then split from. The journey out into the left universe refreshed it and by 1980 it was back home and ready to go it alone again. New theoretical contraptions had to be mocked up in order to mark itself out from what was then a fairly crowded field back on earth.

We pick up the trajectory of Workers' Power, then mainly led by Richard Brenner (who will be voiced by Peter Sallis when he goes into the dark again) in 2013, the year of the SWP rape crisis, something that was to have disastrous consequences for women who were still with the state capitalists, but which also reenergised the young left activists who were beginning to remake connections between socialism and feminism. The question is, of course, Whose close shave? Well, first, it was Left Unity who were unlucky enough to have Workers' Power join them to piss off new members seeking a way out of the sectarian swamp.

Then it was a real possibility of romance that Workers' Power muscled in on and helped mess up; the possible 'regroupment' taking place between different fragments burnt by old-left command and control politics. The key player here was the International Socialist Network which consisted mainly of ex-members of the SWP who had made the first break with their abusive home organisation in 2013, and who were now working closely with the Anticapitalist Initiative (ACI). This is when new avatars of Wendolene, Preston and Shaun come onto the scene, and part of the problem is knowing who is who, who you can trust to be engaging in the discussions in good faith, and who you can't.

Leading members of the ACI had broken from Workers' Power the year before, taking out most of its 'Revolution' youth organisation, but when the ACI and ISN were avidly courted by Socialist Resistance to build a new joint organisation – and it would have been a big step bringing in some of the best of the new activists together – lingering affections for their old comrades led some involved to ask if Workers' Power could tag along; a big mistake, for it meant the end of the regroupment project (something that was not helped by the Socialist Resistance leadership becoming hopelessly enamoured with the newly emerging RS21 during that time).

There was a danger, of course, that Workers' Power could haemorrhage more members to a new joint organisation in the process, and so Richard

Brenner rushed around the country to keep the comrades in line. When Workers' Power were asked if they would continue organising as a separate party inside a future fused organisation, they would robotically repeat that they would wait and see. They had their own escape vehicle almost ready, not completely built, but with the first panels and nuts and bolts stuck together in the form of an unstable rickety ship it called The League for the Fifth International. It was a close shave indeed for the British far left, for a lash up that incorporated them would have ended in the destruction of every other group involved. Those new alliances to expand the Workers' Power household came to naught.

And so we come to *The Wrong Trousers*, in which Richard Brenner was completely trapped inside his Wallace persona, dragging along the rest of the comrades, who, by turns, rolled their eyes at new schemes to build Workers' Power and the Fifth International, and at other times lie doggo until Richard pushed them into action. That was until they spoke up for trans-rights, and anatomically-correct Richard left the group. The 'wrong trousers' in this case is actually a bigger machine, the Labour Party, into which Workers' Power stuck itself after saying goodbye to Left Unity. In it goes, and though they claim to have shut up shop in 2015, click on the Britain tab of the Fifth International site and you will be taken quick as a flash to Red Flag, and there they are proclaiming they are the 'British Section'.

They have trimmed down their programme now, keeping in their pockets their trademark calling card for resistance against Ukraine, which is depicted as a fascist state. You can still work out who is in Workers' Power when they either try to stitch in a tendentious reference to Ukraine in joint platform proposals or react badly if you refer to the Maidan movement as in any way positive or even contradictory; it's the opposite of 'say cheese' to these Wallace and Gromits, don't say 'Ukraine'.

16

SOCIALIST PARTY
OF GREAT BRITAIN

Lars and the Real Girl, a romantic comedy from 2007 directed by Craig Gillespie, brings together two dolls for the lead parts signalled in the title of the film. One is the 'Lars' played, if that is the word, by Ryan Gosling in a typically blank performance, perfect for the role; the other lead is the 'Real Girl' Bianca who doesn't do much acting either but we don't expect her to do much. There is really no single lead, no hero in this film, but a blank robotic space; Lars responds in what is supposed to be stereotypic autistic fashion to encounters with others – this is supposed to be part of the comedy – and is looking for a companion, which is the romantic hook of the film.

There is some cod-psychobabble in the film; we learn that after Lars' mother died all that he had left of her was her scarf which he clutches against his mouth as a kind of comfort-blanket, and it is his loss of mother which, we are led to believe, is at the core of his refusal of relationship with a woman, with others, with community.

Bianca is an anatomically-correct life-size doll that Lars gets mail order after shrinking from a romantic approach by a real real girl Margo (Kelli Garner). Lars backs off from real relationships, he does not like being touched, and we are quickly cued in to some pathological stuff. When Bianca arrives in town and is introduced to the family – key players here are his brother Gus (Paul Schneider) and pregnant sister-in-law Karin (Emily Mortimer) – and to the local parish, he is taken on a pretext to a doctor who diagnoses his 'delusion', the way he fabricates a new reality around the doll. He is isolated, and the community is encouraged to humour him. Pretty predictably, Lars and Margo will get together by the end of the film in what was touted in some reviews as a heart-warming life-affirming paean to the good Christian communities of the US mid-West.

'Bianca is a missionary' Lars tells bewildered friends and family, and says that she is half Danish and half Brazilian. The narrative runs on two tracks: as his sister-in-law comes closer to giving birth, gruff heartless brother Gus, who thinks that humouring Lars over his life-size doll is crazy, comes around and he turns out to have a heart of gold just in time for him to mature into his impending role as a good father; doll Bianca gets 'sick', ends up in hospital, 'dies', and her exit opens the way for Lars to let go of her and find a place in his heart for Margo.

Some of the Christian commentaries on the film were a little worried about the anatomically-correct doll stuff but reassured that Lars was doing the decent thing and that it was clear that he wasn't actually having sex with Bianca, and so they eventually declared it a perfect example of what a loving embrace by a god-fearing community should look like; Lars is spiritually pure, no threat. And, on top of that, of course, once Bianca was in the ground his deviant behaviour eventually gave way to a double heteronormative embrace as Lars matured enough to move onto a concluding tentative relationship with Margo.

SPGB

Lars is a good boy who grows up and might then connect with others. There is no prospect yet of that happening to what has become known to its detractors and ex-members as 'the small party of good boys', the Socialist Party of Great Britain (SPGB). The SPGB pops into the media from time to time, sometimes when journalists confuse them with SPEW (the Socialist Party of England and Wales), and then the party operates as a stand-in for a real Trotskyist group. This is weird because the SPGB are not at all Trotskyist, wary even of calling themselves Marxist. Their 'revolution' will come by way of a parliamentary majority, they claim; more than that, a parliamentary majority in every country in the world.

They've been round the block for longer than most British left groups, mostly around Hyde Park Corner where they hone their skills in winning the working class to socialism, winning one member at a time, recruiting very carefully, and only, the satirist ex-member John Bird disclosed, after passing a test. The SPGB split from the Socialist Democratic Federation back in 1904, and has maintained itself in splendid isolation from the rest of the left ever since, insisting that any other group that wants to engage in joint activity has to sign up to its own complete programme.

Their socialism is 'real socialism' in much the same way as Bianca is a 'real girl' – that is, not at all – constructed as a delusory fantasy which harms no one else around them, and that because it has absolutely no effect on the world. It is an ideal construct completely uncontaminated by anything that actually happens in the real world, and their dwindling membership keeps itself busy evangelising to those who will listen, and writing letters to newspapers about why the solution to this or that problem is socialism now. They have no one leader, that function is a blank space, which means that even Ryan Gosling won't be up for the part. They are governed instead by a ten-man council, and every split away gives rise to another little group –

the short-lived 'Movement for Social Integration' being one case in point – that itself has absolutely nothing to do with the rest of the left and stumbles along in its own little world before it expires (though Joan Lestor, who left during the 'Turner Controversy' in the mid-1950s, did end up as a Labour MP).

The SPGB and a miniscule collection of like-minded parties in other countries (in the World Socialist Movement) are very protective of their Bianca doll-like image of socialism, and have kept with her far longer than Lars did, and along the way they've been able to keep her pure; we can be sure they've never done anything unseemly to her or with her. Like Lars, they don't like to be touched, and they cut themselves off from revolutionary politics over a century ago when they refused to have anything to do with the Russian Revolution. It was merely a 'coup' they say. Instead they cling onto their programme as their little comfort blanket when faced with reality.

Even before the death of the mother of all revolutions in October 1917, which was also the mother of all of the other Marxist groups, the

SPGB had condemned the Irish Easter Rising against British imperialism in 1916 on the basis that it was a violent fragmentation of the unity of the world working class. They opposed the Suffragettes because that movement, they claimed, pitted women against men (the SPGB is mainly composed of men).

They've been true to form ever since; refusing to be involved in anti-fascist struggle (nothing so special about fascism when capitalism is the underlying problem, they say, and anyway, if the fascists were elected by the working-class who are they to poo-poo it); against the Campaign for Nuclear Disarmament (ditto, get rid of capitalism and you deal with the real problem). They, like Lars, are proudly 'impossibilist', that is, they won't have anything to do with reforms to the capitalist system – any reforms will only strengthen and validate capitalism – and the only possible route to socialism is to win everyone over to their ideas, to recruit them into their own view of the world. There is no Margo on the horizon for them.

One of the nice but useless things about the SPGB is that they are about as endearing as Ryan

Gosling if you just face up to the fact that there is nothing beneath the blank face; they don't run front organisations to draw potential members in; they are playing the long game. What you see is what you get, there is nothing else beneath the surface of their programme – you can take it or leave it – and if you humour them and leave them alone they will be happy with their entirely self-constructed ideal 'real socialism', a threat to no one, and no threat at all to the capitalist state.

17

COMMUNIST PARTY OF GREAT BRITAIN (PROVISIONAL CENTRAL COMMITTEE)

Fight Club from 1999 has an unnamed narrator, played by Edward Norton, as the central character. Who is he? He is not all right Jack, not a collective subject, and his wretched life as an alienated individual is not going to get any better in this tale that the director David Fincher once called 'a coming of age story'. It sure is, of a type. Our narrator engages in a fruitless search for recognition in a myriad of self-help support groups in which he learns to spill his guts and talk about his feelings. Here he meets Meat Loaf in a group for victims of testicular cancer and Marla Singer, played by Helena Bonham Carter, as a cynical fellow-traveller who fakes different kinds of symptoms and identities in order to be eligible to join in each of the different groups. These are forms of 'safe space' that are anything but; not refuges from identity but sink-clubs in which identity is relentlessly mined at the very same moment that they make victims of all who join them.

One day, returning from a soul-draining business trip, our narrator swaps gossip with a nice young guy about their similar briefcases, and this spins into a fistfight. This ostensibly nice guy is Tyler Durden, played by Brad Pitt, who inducts Norton into something a little more exciting, more blood and full-body clutches in 'Fight Club'. Fight Club pits itself against the commercialised self-soothing consumerism that is contemporary US-America, and operates as a secret fraternity – these are all men – who fight bare-knuckle and revel in the violence. And so we move into Tyler Durden's underworld of macho homoerotic physical combat in which the men rebel together against consumerism. Up pop Marla and Meat Loaf again, converts to the cause, either as sinister accomplices or place-men, dupes.

The radical shift from consumer society into a world of brutal fistfights flowers in 'Project Mayhem' as a full-blown revolt in which it is unclear who the enemy is and even more uncertain what the progressive alternative will be. There are famously no rules in Fight Club, or, rather, there are many rules which bind it and protect it against the outside world, most important is the repetitive overarching rule that 'You do not talk about Fight Club'.

At the denouement of the film it is unclear who Tyler Durden is exactly, and who the narrator is; Edward Norton's character refers to himself as 'Jack', which one of the many 'explanatory' websites, www.jackdurden.com, picks up on. The narrator says of his saviour and nemesis Tyler Durden 'I am Jack's wasted life', '...smirking revenge', '...complete lack of surprise'; the young men are as glued to each other as much as they fight each other, and the physical violence is both cathartic release from the pressure to be the image of a well-behaved man; an image sold back to them by the advertising industry and deadly trap which basically makes visible the 'obscene underside' of the Law, of hegemonic forms of masculinity (as Slavoj Žižek and his pals would say).

CPGB-PCC

What a journey the key characters in the Communist Party of Great Britain (Provisional Central Committee) (CPGB-PCC) have made since their days in the New Communist Party in the late 1970s, a super-Stalinist split from the old CPBG that was viewed as having gone soft under the influence of Eurocommunism, a historic compromise with consumerism which bore fruit in the rebranding of its magazine *Marxism Today* as an advertising brochure for 'New Times'. The narrator in the weekly podcasts produced by the CPGB-PCC leader John who has taken on the pseudonym 'Jack' – 'Jack Conrad' to signal perhaps his own journey into the heart of darkness – complement a series of videos on the group's website which mainly consist of lean young men aping the lecture style of a combination of urgent sales-man and televangelist.

The standard opening to these little lectures seems to be that you will not be told what you thought the talk was about, but something else. Toying with the audience replicates something of the internal structure of the group. There is some-thing brutal and sad about these advertisements for the party that either parade their cadre or mock those who are desperate to be part of the fun (the video of poor Chris Knight bleating that it is months since he applied for membership and has still not heard anything since being a case in point). At this point, before they went back into the shad-ows, they were the obscene underside of Fight Club, the rule being that 'You must talk about the CPGB-PCC'.

This has been a journey from Stalinism and from attempts to return the old Communist Party of Great Britain to the true path, to what it was when it was the British Section of the Communist International and loyal to Moscow (before the party packed up completely after the failed attempt to rebrand itself as Democratic Left in 1991).

Some weird encounters since those days with some
of the most robotic of the Trotskyist groups – the
CPGB-PCC seems to have learnt something about
politics and organisation from its time with the
Spartacists – have left their mark. The internal life
of the CPGB-PCC as well as its interventions in
other groups unfortunate enough to give them
house-room seems modelled on Tyler Durden's
image of rebellion, with Jack morphing at moments into former IMG member and now party
comrade Mike MacNair who has been hatched
back into politics after his time in Law at St Hugh's
College Oxford. It's not clear now who will be up
to replace Edward and Brad in the remake of Fight
Club, and which one will be which.

It is for their awful intervention in Left Unity
that they will be remembered by many of the rest
of the left, bruised by the experience. Left Unity
was set up to 'do politics differently', but the
CPGB-PCC comrades were having none of that.
Jack and his team seemed to turn every attempt
to make discussion meetings into 'safe spaces' (in
which people new to politics would feel able to
contribute) into, instead, bear gardens. This was

necessary, it was explicitly said by our macho mates, because only those with thick skins would really turn out to be the ones with the mettle to change the world. What was effectively bullying of members of Left Unity inside the meetings was extended to verbatim reports of what the weaklings had said in the CPGB-PCC gossip sheet Weekly Worker – it functioned for a while as the Private Eye of the left – and members of Left Unity used to wait in dread for what would be reported about them, named, for their comrades, work colleagues and bosses to read about them.

The CPGB-PCC was on form, and their comrades sure seemed up for a fight. They left, but not until they had hastened the decline of the organisation, before jumping ship and entering the Labour Party to torment new activists who had looked for something better with Jeremy Corbyn only to be faced with the latest incarnation of this Fight Club of the Left as Labour Party Marxists. They then set up other front organisations such as Labour Left Alliance (after closing down the Labour Party Marxists site), during which time they expelled one of their few remaining female members.

These guys are tough on their enemies and on their friends, and, to their credit, they have dealt firmly and fairly with some pretty unpleasant types who threatened to turn them in some strange new directions; their support for Moshé Machover (who has always denied that he is a member) and their expulsion of Ian Donovan (who found a new home in Socialist Fight) has been exemplary. On the downside, and this where the CPGB-PCC operates as the worst arena for young men to come of age in politics, they have spewed out a stream of dodgy characters who all seem to want to be little Jacks, young men who are confused about what it is to be Tyler Durden and who end up causing mayhem in any other group or campaign they touch.

They were predictable as an internal opposition inside the old CPGB they attempted resurrect from the dead, and predictably bad as a stand-alone alternative. From bad old Stalinism to a form of quasi-Trotskyist politics that repeats all the worst of the organisational practices that Lenin and Trotsky themselves criticised, this lot is one to avoid; those who have been on the sharp end of their politics would say this was a group with a wasted life, smirking revenge and complete lack of surprise.

18

SOCIALIST EQUALITY PARTY

La La Land released in 2016 was a musical comedy romance filmed against a backdrop of violence that was both implicit in the film itself and in the directorial history that preceded it. The film shot into the headlines, first in the flash of hype which successfully publicised its launch, and made out that it was a more substantial reflection of Hollywood life than the light froth it turned out to be, and then in the embarrassed mistaken announcement of best picture award at the Oscars through which it almost eclipsed the success of the black and queer film *Moonlight*.

Just as much as *Moonlight* was about the weight of history, about the multiple forms of oppression that condition contemporary politics, so La La Land was about the erasure of history and its replacement with a glossy surface and the pretence that an image of success should be enough to win out in the end, even if that was a bitter-sweet image of success haunted by the regret of its two main characters at their actual failure to make it into the big time.

The film traces the interwoven wannabe-celebrity life trajectories of Emma Stone as 'Mia Dolan', and Ryan Gosling as 'Sebastian Wilder'. They meet and fight and part and meet again in a sequence of elaborate dance numbers that conjure up the heyday of the entertainment industry they themselves want to break into. There are a number of faux-reflexive reminders that they really are actors, including their own film date when they see *Rebel Without a Cause* before going to the planetarium which also features in that classic film. Emma wants to be an actress, which entails a running pretend in-joke for the audience as she struggles at auditions and then fails with her own one-woman show. Ryan, meanwhile, wants to perform at his own jazz club, for which he is eventually rewarded with a cringe-making final scene in which he hosts and stars at the piano as a nice white guy surrounded by black musicians as his employees (and that involves a darker joke in which Ryan replicates the recuperation of jazz by white mass culture and sidelining of its black history).

The opening scene has Mia and Sebastian enacting a first missed encounter during a traffic jam on a Los Angeles highway, during which the first big stage number 'Another Day of Sun' sees drivers leaping from their cars and dancing across the bonnets and roofs as they sing of their aspiration to make it in Hollywood and of unfulfilled dreams. One cannot watch this six-minute single take – fake, it turns out, for it was stitched together from three separate shots with some clever cuts – without thinking that these poor saps pouring their hearts into the opening number are the self-same characters they are performing, a very postmodern replication of what is represented that most Marxist critics hated. Class is pretty much missing from the film, replaced with aspiration, a self-admiring film about two narcissists who we are supposed to sob over when they are unable to get it together.

As well as this implicit symbolic violence in the texture of the film, there is the violent quasi-prequel in the director Damien Chazelle's *Whiplash* two years earlier which stages sadistic coaching of a jazz student in which the message is no pain no gain, lots of pain and humiliation.

SEP

The big oft-repeated accusation in the mainstream media against revolutionary Marxists is that they live in some kind of La La Land, doomed to hope for somewhere over the rainbow where their dream of another world beyond capitalism might come about, and it is unfortunately true that some left groups do actually already seem to live there. Some groups really do fit the bill, hallucinating into existence a version of the world as they would like it to be so their own version of Marxism can be made to appear foolproof. Meet the Socialist Equality Party (SEP) and the World Socialist Web Site (WSWS), formed out of the ruins of what was once one of the largest Trotskyist groups in Britain, the Workers Revolutionary Party (WRP) led by Gerry Healy – a plum part for Ryan Gosling coming up – who danced on the international stage of far-left politics until the mid-1980s with his best friend Vanessa Redgrave, who will one day perhaps be played by Emma Stone. They have gone their different ways now – Gerry to the great Fourth International in the sky, and Vanessa in other political and artistic directions (with fanfare launches of the now defunct 'Marxist Party' and then the 'Peace and Progress Party').

Those were the days. Those old WRP years were years of steady industrial implantation from its formation as 'The Club' in 1947 which was encouraged by the Fourth International (FI) to split from the Revolutionary Communist Party (then the British section of the FI) and work inside the Labour Party. The Club recruited leading Communist Party activists after the Soviet invasion of Hungary in 1956, and then announced a jazzier new name, the 'Socialist Labour League' in 1959 before its final incarnation as the WRP in 1973. By that time the WRP had already broken from the Fourth International to become a key player in its own 'International Committee of the Fourth International' (ICFI) in 1953, and it then refused to take part in the reunification of the FI in 1963. It was from that experience that it hallucinated into existence its favourite bugbear 'Pabloism' (the programmatic line named after Michel Pablo, that the FI should participate in larger organisations in order to win activists to socialism).

That old WRP is not to be confused, SEP and WSWS supporters will remind you, with the treacherous splitters of the present-day so-called fake rival WRP which still publishes the old WRP newspaper '*News Line*' (founded in 1976 as successor to '*Workers Press*'). The SEP insists that it and it alone is the ICFI, as do the current WRP. The disintegration of the WRP was a tragic, slow-burning spectacle staged for the rest of the left through the 1970s and then dramatically fast in 1985. Fantasy displaced reality as the WRP turned into a kind of cult, and Gerry Healy began to give lectures on 'dialectics' during which a correct Marxist account of the world was advanced to explain, for example, that there could not possibly have been a revolution in Cuba because there was no revolutionary party there.

The rest of the British far left knew there were serious problems, that the glittery promises of the WRP to its actor members that they would have their own clubs were empty. Corin Redgrave had bought them White Meadows Villa in Derbyshire in 1975 for 'training', but finance also came from the brutal regimes in Iraq and Libya in return for favourable coverage in its press. 1976 saw the launch of the WRP 'Security and the Fourth International' investigation and a campaign which saw a stepping up of violence against other groups that were viewed as complicit in the death of Trotsky. This crazy conspiracy theory carries on today in the fevered imagination of the Socialist Equality Party and in WSWS accusations against rival groups.

The WRP industrial base was bit by bit eclipsed by the influx of revolutionary luvvies attracted by the passion for Gerry Healy by Vanessa Redgrave and her brother Corin who at one point made serious inroads into the actors union 'Equity'. Equity members who joined the WRP would then get a taste of the humiliation that had been metered out to other petty bourgeois types; well, actually to anyone who disagreed with Gerry, and some of them seemed to enjoy it. It might be a public tongue-lashing or, if you were lucky, you might even be slapped by the great man. The all-singing all-dancing dream crashed as the violence came to a head in revelations that Gerry Healy had sexually abused young women in the organisation during what the British tabloid press called the 'Red in the Bed' events.

They were all already heading for La La Land, whether that included buying Trotsky's death-mask and displaying it at rallies, or using Richard Burton's photo as Trotsky in public literature in place of a picture of the real thing. Today the SEP and WSWS lurches from fantasy to fantasy, including bizarre reflexively ironic attacks on postmodernism, which they now seem to hate almost as much as Pabloism. They were once a serious industrial force and did good anti-racist work which won black youth to their party, but now all the SEP and WSWS really seems to rebel against is the rest of the left, and reality has been left far behind.

19

SOCIALIST ACTION

Michael Powell and Emeric Pressburger's 1948 classic The Red Shoes is one of their best films. This was another fruit of their writer-producer-director partnership, one that starred Marius Goring as Julian Craster, a composer hopelessly in love with Moira Shearer (as Victoria Page, the ballet dancer carried away by the red shoes) who is lured away, eventually to her death, by impresario Anton Walbrook (as Boris Lermentov).

As with many films, what goes on off-set is as indicative of the underlying and most significant narrative of the film as what appears on the screen. And it is only after the event that viewers can better reframe what they have seen and make sense of what is going on. In this case it is Marius Goring who is one of those centre-stage, bewitched by the dancer with the red shoes, and in a tense rivalrous relationship with Walbrook, but given a role by his rival as répétiteur with the ballet after it has become clear that he, Marius Goring, was the composer of some excellent pieces that had been passed off as the work of another.

No rebel is Marius, though; off-screen he was one of the key players in the British actor's trade union 'Equity' after having been a founding member in 1929, and president of it from 1963 to 1965 and from 1975 to 1982. A great actor but a reactionary political actor, attempting to break the union boycott of apartheid South Africa, and at war with the left who were mainly organised by then influential Workers Revolutionary Party before the WRP collapsed after the Gerry Healy 'red in the bed' scandal.

Marius Goring is a real unrecognised genius in the film, watching with horror the love of his life expire, but in real life joins the camp of those in power. One might say that just as it is Moira Shearer who is captured by the beautiful red shoes who dance their way to her demise, so it is Marius Goring who is captured by political forces that he thought he could control. The narrative that flows from the film into real life is one in which a clever writer is tempted by the promise of influence and ends up at the mercy of the objects of his love.

SA

All this takes a little decoding, something that is equally the case for the shadowy group Socialist Action that once imagined that it had influence in the British Labour Party but ended up becoming a creature of the apparatus, a group led by figures who were tempted by the lure of influence in the Chinese Communist Party but ended up as propagandists for the Stalinist tradition they were once so cleverly critical of. Much as you might like Socialist Action, you won't find out how to join through its website or its members, but you might get a lucky tap on the shoulder and be invited in one day if you can prove how enamoured you are of it.

The group is a sorry residue of the decision by the International Marxist Group, IMG, then British section of the Fourth International, to enter the Labour Party in 1982, changing its name to the 'Socialist League' in the process as cover, and folding up its paper *Socialist Challenge*, replacing it with its own tabloid and then eventually, from 1988 a magazine called *Socialist Action*. A three-way war broke out, with one group vying for the affections of the Fourth International, succeeding and so splitting away in 1985; this was the group that eventually, after several more splits, mutations and fusions with some fragments of the old WRP, became Socialist Resistance. Another group, acolytes of Jack Barnes' US-American-based Pathfinder Tendency, nearly succeeded in seizing control, but was expelled in 1988, to become the Communist League.

The Fourth International and Pathfinder Tendency which was run by what was effectively once the American section of the Fourth International are the two red shoes. What was left was the third group run by a prominent former leader and theoretician of the IMG John Ross. It is John Ross who would be played by Marius Goring in a film of these times. A very clever guy, sometimes a bit of a demagogue, author of key IMG texts under his own name and under a pseudonym 'Alan Jones', he wanted a new arena, new company in which he could exert some influence. After having watched his red shoes dance his old partners away, he searched around for replacements. There were two options, both of which are visible in the present-day productions of Socialist Action. In the process, the women, as is so often the case in left groups, disappear from the scene. There is no Moira Shearer in this story. It is Marius Goring who is the focus of attention.

One red shoe was and still is the British Labour Party; apparatchiks from Socialist Action burrowed their way into Ken Livingstone's Greater London Council, GLC, and several of them, including John Ross, functioning as advisors and authors of key policy documents. This was one machine that ran away with them, carrying them far away from their old Trotskyist roots into social-democratic administration. Livingstone had actually appeared on a *Socialist Challenge* platform with Ernest Mandel from the Fourth International as speaker shortly after becoming leader of the GLC, and most members of the IMG were in the

Labour Party way before its transformation into the Socialist League in 1982.

Lurid stories appeared in the London mainstream press as late as 2002 fingering Ken Livingstone's 'policy directors' Redmond O'Neill and John Ross, both of Socialist Action. This, we were told, was Livingstone's 'Praetorian Guard'. Ross is said to have courted capitalists in the City of London on Livingstone's behalf, and raced back to London to be his economic advisor during the mayoral race, from Moscow where he was advising financial institutions about how to negotiate the new capitalist reality after the fall of the Wall. He is described as a 'jovial man', one picture of him that IMG members will remember.

And then, it is from Moscow to Beijing. The other red shoe that was dangled in front of the group was the fabulous economic success of the Chinese regime, and so a regime that had imprisoned and murdered Trotskyists became academic and political home for Ross, who now pushes out remarkable defences of the bureaucracy. Now Ross is Senior Fellow at Chongyang Institute for Financial Studies, Renmin University, and it is from that platform that he firmly denies that China is capitalist. This leads him to defend the regime, and then, just as loyally, to line up with the regime against the protesters in Hong Kong.

In Powell and Pressburger's film *The Red Shoes*, the ballet company and the internal alliances and intrigues in that company are as important as the machinations of director, if not more so. This is a company firmly rooted on the European continent; the final action takes place in Italy, and the film was shot in England and France. The allure of continental Europe was always important to the IMG, and to Ross; that was always part of the appeal of the Fourth International to British Trotskyists. Now Ross's group Socialist Action has simply transferred its affections to a much bigger continental landmass, China, one that paints itself red, and has Ross to help them do that, but in the process he has painted himself into a corner. His enthusiasm has run away with him and led him far away from his first loves, and from socialism itself.

20

COMMUNIST
LEAGUE

One of the most striking things about Lars von Trier's 2008 film *The Boss of It All* is not so much the plot as the way it was made, and then the weird disorienting effect it has on the viewer as they try to work out what is going on. Everyone in the company is trying to work out what is going on, and who is in charge. That's the crux of the plot really. The real head of a Danish IT company, Ravn (played by Peter Gantzler), has been outsourcing all the bad and unpopular management decisions to a fictional 'Boss of it all' somewhere overseas for years, and that means he doesn't take the flak when things go wrong. But now when he wants to sell the company to some Icelandic guys, they want to meet the real big boss to sign the handover documents, and so Ravn hires Kristoffer (Jens Albinus) to play the part. When they encounter Kristoffer, different members of the company play out their own fantasies and theories about what kind of guy he is, assuming, for example that the dopier he seems the more brilliant a manager he actually is, and so on.

It's a bit of a shaggy dog story from Trier, better known for his more disturbing erratic off-the-wall films. It all looks innocent enough, but, given his past form, we are always expecting this farce to slide into something worse. And there are some nice barely hidden subplots in the film, with the Icelandic buyers at one moment making demands to see the main man and, behaving like US American corporate asset-strippers – that gives a particular frisson of fear to the company staff who don't know what the transfer of management-ownership betokens – and at the next behaving like upstart entrepreneurs. Remember that Iceland is a former colony of Denmark, and so there are old historical master-slave dynamics at work at different levels of this deception.

The company employees are being duped about who really runs the show, but this uncertainty about what the film is really about is replicated in the production process. Von Trier repeatedly suddenly 'jump cuts' from one scene to another, and the film, critics have pointed out, has an 'uncannily detached feel and anaesthetically flat look'. At the same time, there are shifts in image and sound so that there is a sense of ventriloquism at work: bits of dialogue are assembled as if from different places, and so it is not clear at any moment who is really speaking, or, more to the point, who is speaking beyond or behind or through another character.

CL

So it is with the bit part members of the Communist League, who have managed to keep the show on the road in Britain since they were ejected from a more mysterious and deliberately secretive group, Socialist Action, in 1988. They will show up at demonstrations and unfold a bookstall with some very old pamphlets and copies of their newspaper;

well, not their own newspaper, but one put together by the big boss over the pond, *The Militant*. *The Militant* was founded back in 1928, and is the public voice of the Socialist Workers Party in the United States, and every twist and turn of this once-significant force on the US-American left is dictated by Jack Barnes and relayed to followers in the so-called 'Pathfinder Tendency' around the world, including to the Communist League franchise here in the UK.

Jack Barnes was elected National Secretary of the Party in 1972, and has clung onto power ever since. The American SWP was effectively the section of the Fourth International (though prohibited from officially declaring itself to be such, as it reminded readers of its pamphlets and books in a phrase pasted in as a footnote in every text, by the reactionary Voorhis Act), but the party under Barnes' leadership finally broke from the Fourth International in 1990 after some bizarre attempts to make Fidel Castro boss of it all. Then there is a strange and sad political journey, from debates over independent revolutionary strategy in Latin America to cheer-leading the Cuban leadership whatever it does, from leading worker protests through the Teamsters Union in the US, to hailing the victory of Trump in the presidential election and then siding with the right-wing libertarian Trump protesters against COVID-19 lockdown, and from principled support for the Palestinians to welcoming the re-election of Netanyahu and explicitly supporting Israel.

You can't understand what the Communist League is up to unless you are au fait with the twists and turns of the Barnes group, now a shadow of its former self, and its publishing arm Pathfinder Press. But wait a minute, things aren't as they first seem. President of Pathfinder Press is Mary-Alice Waters, Jack Barnes' partner, and the actual ownership of these entities seems vested in the Anchor Foundation, which sold off the SWP headquarters in Manhattan for an eye-watering sum, 20 million dollars. The legal tangle of share ownership of different aspects of the controlling stake in the Pathfinder Tendency and the paper and pamphlets, including propaganda that the Communist League hawk around the place in the UK, is pretty complicated. Every revolutionary group has to manoeuvre its finances to escape the gaze of the capitalist state, but that is not the point now. Now it is not clear who indeed is the Boss of it all, and who benefits. This is what stokes accusations that Barnes and Walters are running a business and sit in the most expensive seats at the New York opera.

Back to the Communist League, in bad company and following Barnes every step of the way. Back in the day, in the 1970s, Jonathan Silberman, who leads the Communist League, would regale members of the International Marxist Group, IMG, with stories of his motorcycle journeys across the US to attend the SWP congress in Oberlin, Ohio. Then Barnes' supporters would operate in Britain inside the British section of the Fourth International, IMG, as the 'Leninist Trotskyist Faction', and a small group of Canadians ran the Pathfinder Bookshop in The Cut near Waterloo Station south of the Thames in London. What was crucial to their success was winning IMG leaders Brian Grogan and John Ross to support them. The fatal blow was struck by Barnes insisting on a 'turn to industry' that effectively destroyed many sections of the Fourth International for a while, including in Britain.

When the IMG changed its name to the Socialist League, went into the Labour Party and disintegrated, Socialist Action appeared as its best organised successor organisation; Ross broke from Grogan to continue with Socialist Action. The Barnes group had held on as long as they could, even winning a majority just before a conference, but the writing was on the wall, and out they went. Today they are reduced to being little more than a joke item in the bourgeois press, including the rabidly anti-Corbyn *Jewish Chronicle*, who didn't know quite what to make of a self-declared communist standing for London mayor.

The giveaway about the Communist League's political allegiances comes in rather odd references to support for 'workers and farmers', a legacy of the call for 'workers and farmers' governments everywhere, particularly Cuba. Candidates pop up in different places every now and again, in London, in Edinburgh, and in Manchester, to get derisory votes even less than random mistakes in the polling booth. Today, it is unclear which actors, Peter

Gantzler or Jens Albinus, would play Barnes and Silberman in a dramedy based on the trajectory of the Pathfinder Tendency. What is clear is that the Communist League are playing supporting roles to Barnes. Silberman for one has certainly been taken for a ride, and anyone who joins them is going to go nowhere fast.

21

WORKERS
REVOLUTIONARY
PARTY

Only a film as weird as Carlos Vermut's 2018 *Quién Te Cantará* will do justice to the key question we are often posed when we see or read something, and wonder who it is for and who it is by. This is a film as much about the audience who is to be witness to the performance, as it is about the performer and what they are trying to tell us. While 'quién te cantará' translates from Spanish most literally as 'who will sing to you', and the identity of the singer is clearly at issue here, one might most properly interpret the meaning of the phrase in the context of the film as 'who is it that is singing to you (and who would you be that they are singing to you)'.

Famous singer Lila, played by Najwa Nimri, is a pop star who hasn't sung for ten years and is about to make a comeback when she has an accident while swimming in the sea and loses her memory, including remembering how to sing. So, an avid fan Violeta (played by Eva Llorach) who performs a tribute act to Lila in a small-town bar is enrolled in the secret task of singing for her, singing to her, reminding her who she, Lila was, who she is. The story does and does not have a happy end (spoiler alert) depending on which Lila you are; Lila the star who does appear on stage in a successful performance or the would-be Lila who walks slowly to her death in the sea at the end of the film.

There is a sub-text of simmering violence, including, crucially between Violeta and her daughter Marta (played by Natalia Molina), and the small town on the coast where the film is shot is called 'Rota' which, as some admiring and critical reviews have pointed out, could be both the name of the place and a descriptor of 'broken woman'. This is one of those rare films about relationships between women, with very few men on the scene, and about women, who they are when they must perform to others.

WRP

A key question for anyone who stumbles across the Workers Revolutionary Party today is, Who reads their daily newspaper *News Line*, and who are they that would produce and sell this thing? That there is a daily newspaper of the revolutionary left in Britain is still quite incredible, but it is now only on odd occasions that the thing pops into view; in a public square in Manchester, for example, when the old-timers on their collapsible chairs admit that they have travelled over from Leeds to sell it even though they claim to have hundreds of members in the city; or in the centre of London late on a deserted dark night outside a University library; or, most alarmingly during the COVID-19 crisis, on a street in the East End of London knocking door to door to sell the paper.

Once upon a time the answer was clear, if not to the readers at least to the members of the WRP, then the largest Trotskyist organisation in Britain who were convinced that if they were not on the brink of power, they were at the edge of the cliff, at the point in history when there would either be socialism (under their leadership, for any other version could not be socialism at all) or barbarism. Many branches of the WRP, those that did not consist of resting actors battling for leadership of their trade union Equity, had a family-clan structure, with kids around the country enrolled into the desperate and unceasing task of cycling to the railway station late at night, every night, and then delivering warnings of impending dictatorship if there was no revolution. Gerry Healy led the outfit and succeeded in recruiting working class families, and some prominent actors into his party that started as The Club in 1947, became the Socialist Labour League in 1959 and blossomed into the WRP in 1973.

The ten-year division of the Fourth International from 1953 to 1963 saw Healy's group recognised as one of the halves of the International when the division began. Healy led the so-called 'International Committee of the Fourth International', ICFI, a designation the WRP and *News Line*, retains for its almost non-existent network of sister organisations in different countries to the present-day. The reunification of the Fourth International in 1963 was, predictably, an incomplete one, and the SLL, as it then was, stayed out, battling for what it continued to call the 'ICFI' on the world stage. It was then obsessively pitted against the 'United Secretariat', the USFI which was led for many years by the Marxist economist Ernest Mandel, an International Healy branded as 'Pabloite' (after FI secretary Michel Pablo, even if there were actually few self-declared 'Pabloites' around).

The time for not one, but two, and then many Workers Revolutionary Parties came in 1985, when Gerry Healy was expelled, basically for sexually assaulting over twenty women in the party, and then Corin and Vanessa Redgrave were expelled for supporting him. Here indeed there was a subtext of simmering violence against women in the group, and desperate attempts to remind Healy what he was once was, what he should be as a revolutionary leader instead of a mere abusive crook.

Different editions of *News Line* reported that Healy had been expelled and that he hadn't – a case of Schrodinger's trot – and the two different fragments then each published versions of the newspaper for a while. One fragment eventually mutated into the Socialist Equality Party, while another was still headed by Gerry Healy and Sheila Torrance, one of the few women still loyal to the old brute. Healy and the Redgraves then, in the name of the ICFI, expelled people who produced *News Line* and formed the 'Marxist Party' in 1987 oriented to the Soviet Union (a very untimely move, in retrospect) before dissolving after Healy's death and re-emerging as the 'Peace and Progress Party' before disappearing into the wilderness.

There are actually very few people in the film *Quién Te Cantará*, and they move around quite deserted bare settings as they attempt to act out and re-establish the lives they once had, trying to remember how and why they once did what they did, and who they are. This is a very miserable and reduced game of doubling and identification, each character pretending to be someone they are not. This was a situation that ends in tragic violence, with women suffering, as they so often do at the hands of male leaders in corrupted sectarian left groups that become little worlds enclosed and closed in on themselves.

So, we are left with Sheila Torrance still claiming that her WRP and her newspaper *News Line* is the real deal, and she continues the well-established Healy tradition of feting Arab dictators (something Healy's WRP was willing to do in return for hard cash, but which Torrance does now, it seems, for free). What Torrance is doing in keeping the Healy legacy alive is anyone's guess, and who she is doing it for is an even bigger question.

Healy himself met his maker a while ago now, and, fortunately, there hasn't been another quite like him to take his place, thank goodness. Gerry Healy was no Lila, no superstar, even if the Redgraves and the rest of the gang treated him like one, and so it will be Eva Llorach who will be condemned one day to play Sheila Torrance on the big screen, Sheila mimicking the lines of Gerry's ghost. All that is left is the name of his pretend 'International', the ICFI, and Torrance as the sad reminder and remainder who keeps it going, as nothing, for no one.

22

INTERNATIONAL SOCIALIST LEAGUE

The very short unfinished film of the very big classic book *Moby Dick* was made by Orson Welles in 1971. He wrote it, directed it and took all the roles. This 21-minute film has a history, of course. Welles had appeared in the John Huston 1956 version of Herman Melville's novel as Father Mapple, an ex-whaler who gives a stirring sermon, about what Ishmael will face when he goes to sea. The novel is great; all you want to know about whales is crammed in there. It is as obsessed with whales as is Captain Ahab who searches out the great white whale Moby Dick.

The novel has spawned a whole industry of literary interpretation, with the whale functioning as metaphor for what both drives and pulls us, and as an object lesson in obsessional lusting, both for revenge against what has deprived us of what we once were and for something that will make us whole, fully-present in the world. The whale stands both for nature that must be tamed, brought under control, subdued, and for the highest cultural goals, emblem of success. In the meantime, we plot and rage and seize every opportunity to convey to others the importance of our quest. That is precisely why it would have been such a spectacle, authentic to the book, to have the same actor play the crew-member Ishmael, the sermonising Father Mapple and the main protagonist Ahab.

What better actor-director than Orson Welles to take charge of this, and how great he would have been as Captain Ahab, driving his ship through the sea in search of the object cause of his desire, willing the crew on, taking them through the perilous journey. Orson Welles' 1971 film, if it had been finished, could have taken us way beyond the John Huston version, and we would then really have had a driving force, with the energy not only to guide and lead the mission but to be present in every figure that appears onscreen, in full charge of what was going on.

ISL

Revolution is not yet in sight for the crew of the International Socialist League, ISL, but their doughty leader Martin Ralph guides them from the port of Liverpool, and has much larger ambitions than just taking Old Swan ward in Wavertree constituency. His 'international' is the LIT, of which the ISL proudly declares itself to be the British section. We in Britain should really translate that Latin-America-based network as the 'International Workers League', but the Liga Internacional de los Trabajadores (Cuarta Internacional), is usually known by members and ex-members alike simply as 'the LIT'. Even the ISL is usually known as the LIT, or often hereabouts as 'the Ralph International'.

It has a few members, and does some quite good work locally, but Martin Ralph is the guiding light, a driving force, so much so that it appears to outsiders to be a one-man band, even when Ralph appears at local events with groups of Brazilian visitors in tow, or makes amazing claims about the even more amazing numbers his group has leading the masses across Latin America.

The LIT are 'Morenoites', a species of Trotskyist we don't often encounter in the UK, though occasionally in the North West in the form of Martin Ralph. Nahuel Moreno from Argentina was a larger than life buccaneering figure who joined the United Secretariat of the Fourth International, USFI, at the crucial reunification congress in 1963, but fell out with them after a crazy adventure during the Nicaraguan revolution when he organised the disastrous 'Simon Bolivar International Brigade' to go and fight with the Sandinistas in the 1980s civil war, something the Sandinistas were explicitly advising against. The British Section of the Fourth International, the IMG, expelled a few Morenoites in 1980 organised as the 'Bolshevik Faction Group'.

The Morenoite LIT picked up its 'British section' from the meltdown of the Workers Revolutionary Party that ran its own 'International

Committee of the Fourth International', ICFI. In 1988 a group led by Bill Hunter, who is no longer with us, and Martin Ralph emerged from the wreckage. Nahuel Moreno was a big man, an energetic and controlling figure in Latin America with global ambitions, and Martin Ralph is now one of the best suited to stepping into his shoes, at least around Liverpool. Orson Welles would be a fine choice to play both Moreno and Ralph.

Martin Ralph is well-known for never letting go once he gets hold of the microphone at a meeting; when he was advised by a comrade once that this might be counter-effective, he replied straightaway that revolutionaries need to seize every opportunity to give their message and speak for as long as possible. The Martin Ralph international in Britain it was that, along with Bob Myers, another old WRP-hand, steered the 'Workers Aid for Bosnia' outfit in the 1990s, building a base in the North West. So significant it was that Alan Thornett, from the group that became Socialist Resistance (and so in the USFI tradition of Trotskyism that the ICFI always pitted itself against and that Moreno had fallen out with over his intervention in Nicaragua) came to Manchester to try and mediate between Workers Aid for Bosnia and another broader alliance 'International Workers Aid for Bosnia', IWA. The mediation might have worked because Thornett was once upon a time in the WRP with Bob and Martin, but that might have antagonised them even more. It failed.

We knew that the hopes for a regroupment of the far-left in 2013 were really scuppered when a few groups, including Socialist Resistance, came together for talks but Martin Ralph turned up at a Manchester meeting. He was unusually quiet at the meeting, and it was Workers' Power who were the real destructive element, but it was a powerful indication that the vultures were circling to pick up as many pieces as possible from the resulting quarrels. The enthusiastic participation of the Martin Ralph International in Left Unity was always a liability, one of the tiny sects that fed upon that broad alliance. He is a nice guy, but he carries with him the ambition and energy of Nahuel Moreno, and his single-minded full-on revolutionary programme interventions have their sights on the big prize, nothing less than the big prize now.

This Captain Ahab of the left is the LIT in Britain, and for that his efforts to build the world Trotskyist movement should be acknowledged, if for no other reason than that the Moreno tradition will one day need to play a part again in joint efforts to seek out Revolution, our own big whale. For the moment, though, the ISL is a very little and unfinished project.

23

SOCIALIST FIGHT

Taxi Driver, the 1976 classic film directed by Martin Scorsese and starring Robert De Niro as Travis Bickle, was apparently as seedy in its making as it was in its depiction of its anti-hero. The film became a source of oft-repeated motifs – 'you talkin' to me?' – and became a classic because it eventually spun itself out in cine-history as a string of clichés. It was a lesson in how to dredge around in alienated inner-city life and serve up the mess on-screen as entertainment, an indictment and replication of a sick world which produces sick characters who thrash around trying to make sense of it, taking it out on the wrong guys.

Travis Bickle is the discharged US-Marine after the end of the Vietnam war who sinks into a spiral of depression and paranoia and ends up as a vigilante who takes on the self-appointed role of city cleaner, cleaning the urban landscape of the scum who feed and feed on the rotting society which surrounds him. This context is also the perfect feeding ground for a weird mixture of narcissism – you lookin' at me – and conspiracy theories which systematically misrecognise and mis-locate the cause of evil in the world.

The film traces Bickle's journey from dalliance with big politics to his eventual isolation in the tiniest imaginable sect politics – his own ruminations on power and sleaze and what needs to be done to put it right – and, disconnected from reality, he goes in for the kill. After a failed attempt to assassinate the Senator whose campaign team he was briefly part of, he heads for a brothel where there is a shoot-out, and finally, through lucky chance, he hits out at other characters that public opinion also views as vermin, and turns up lucky.

The film successfully mixes the mistaken and dangerous emerging worldview of an outsider – Travis Bickle doesn't really have a plan or know where he is going – with a series of stereotypes, of sex and race and corruption and crime, systemic misrepresentations of the nature of capitalist society, society that provokes and welcomes his erratic and destructive acting out.

SF

His is a lonesome fight which wallows in ideology, enacting and confirming it, just as it is in the case of Socialist Fight, one of the tiniest of splinters from the nine-way fragmentation of the old Workers Revolutionary Party (WRP) in the 1980s. In this case, the replay of taxi driver Travis Bickle's journey round the edge of politics will entail a contest for the Robert De Niro role between Gerry Downing and Ian Donovan.

Downing, not to be confused with Gerry Healy (though that little Gerry was once the big man for our future star), has written reams about the break-up of the WRP, and he will surely beat Donovan for the role, but this time in a rather more downbeat version of the film, 'Bus Driver' perhaps. Socialist Fight, which proclaims itself to be the British Section of the 'Liaison Committee for the Fourth International' (with three other appendages), is the latest incarnation of Downing after his Workers International League and its paper 'Workers Action' hit the buffers. Donovan, meanwhile, has form in many different roles, having been through more far-left groups than you have had hot dinners, and he'll get a bit part. Just as he does now in Downing's Socialist Fight, which briefly gave Donovan a home following his well-deserved expulsion from the CPGB-PCC. The film-score, by the way, will be by jazz saxophonist and antisemite Gilad Atzmon.

Well, one thing we learn from the spectacle of Downing and Donovan splitting with the rest of the left is that unfortunately there sure is antisemitism on the left too. This is not surprising given that antisemitism still swills around contemporary culture, but revolutionary socialists who take this seriously have been to the forefront of struggles against it. The Socialist Fight version of what August Bebel called the 'socialism of fools' is no less dangerous for being all the more ridiculous. Socialist Fight has already marked itself out on the far-left and alienated many comrades willing to ally with Downing by declaring, for example, that Islamic State is not all bad, and so Downing and Donovan's protestations that they do not at all see themselves to be antisemitic now already ring pretty hollow.

It is to the credit of other left groups involved in the campaign Labour Against the Witch-hunt (LAW) that they are having none of this nonsense. LAW, which was set up to defend, among others, Moshé Machover from accusations of antisemitism, quite rightly draws a sharp line between criticism of Israel – a principled anti-Zionist position in solidarity with the Palestinian people – and the half-baked racist ramblings that Donovan came up with in the CPGB-PCC before he was given the push (by Machover) and that Downing has been pushing in Socialist Fight.

In the tiny narcissistic and paranoiac world of Socialist Fight, there is a 'Jewish Bourgeoisie' that has intimate direct ties to the State of Israel, and it is this conspiratorial vision of the world that supposedly explains why the Jews who are, we are told, 'over-represented' in the ruling class must be called out. Full-blown 'anti-Zionism' must, according to Downing and Donovan, name this Jewish bourgeoisie as an influence to be rooted out, and so (as many hard-line Zionists would predict and wish) anti-Zionism shades into antisemitism.

Downing will have difficulty rowing his way back from this position after Donovan declared that the Jewish bourgeoisie is the main enemy, and the two of them now can't decide whether they hate those Jews more than they hate each other, a matter that was not resolved by Downing expelling Donovan (or vice versa, depending on whose account you read). This is no longer socialism as such, and merely led to two rival 'Socialist Fight' groups, tiny mirror images of each other. No wonder these two were admired by Gilad Atzmon who has made a disgusting speciality of celebrating self-hatred – a Jew who hates, he says, every bit of him that reminds him that he is Jewish – and no wonder that they return the favour.

This is a time of strange but necessary alliances, among which the most important are those alliances of anti-Zionists in the Labour Party that refuse to pander to antisemitism. Many Jews on the left have a proud history of standing out against the Israeli State, protesting against the attempts of Zionists to invoke some weird kind of collective responsibility in which all Jews are expected to fall in line and keep silent for fear of being labelled antisemitic. Moshé Machover is one, an old Trotskyist with a lifetime of resistance to Zionism inside Israel and then outside it, and Tony Greenstein is another (the latter having also written scorching attacks in the CPGB-PCC press on Downing and Donovan), both active members of Labour Against the Witch-hunt.

It is imperative that the new doppelgangers for Travis Bickle are not given the opportunity to fight their way into this campaign again, nor to be given comfort by those who deliberately or unwittingly misunderstand what the stakes are and make them seem as if they are in any way victims of a witch-hunt or heroes as they thrash around looking for someone to blame for their isolation on the left. They reflect the worst of the society they think they pit themselves against. Their fight, let's be clear, is not at all a socialist fight.

24

SPARTACIST LEAGUE

Silence, Martin Scorsese's 2016 historical drama, shows the search by Portuguese Jesuit missionaries for Cristóvão Ferreira, a real-life early seventeenth-century missionary who was captured and tortured in Japan and renounced his faith. The film begins with two young priests who hear with disbelief about this apostasy and decide to set off to Japan to find Ferreira, played by Liam Neeson, and discover the truth. The film traces their voyage to Japan and then their encounters with villagers who have converted to Christianity before being tracked down and punished by the authorities.

Along the way, the priests learn something about the forms of resistance to local power that Christianity keys into in Japanese villages, and about the local forms of belief that might, they conclude, provide the natives with access to a God that is, perhaps, as authentic as that offered by the Jesuits.

A crisis point of faith and redemption in the film comes when Sebastião Rodrigues (played by Andrew Garfield), a character based on the real-life missionary Giuseppe Chiara, hears the voice of Christ telling him that the apostasy demanded of him by the Samurai is justified, that it is Christian in fact, because it will thereby save the lives of others that he hears being tortured for their faith. The film is a complex theological as well as historical depiction of the role that Christianity played when the Jesuits in the seventeenth century functioned as the Pope's foreign agents determined to install the rule of the Catholic Church around the world.

SL

There is no such crisis of faith on the part of members of the Spartacist League when they arrive on foreign shores. The 'Spartacist League / Britain' was formed in 1978, but they no longer even have an independent web presence in Britain. Their publicity operations are handled direct from the US, and this might be because, just as they specialise in provoking splits in rival groups, they are susceptible to divisions and periodic purges in their own ranks. The 'Sparts' as they are not affectionately known (and there are audible groans of recognition from the rest of the left when they turn up outside a target meeting to pitch their stall) have their origins inside the US section of the Fourth International in the early 1960s.

They are Trotskyists of a peculiar kind, quick to leap to the defence of the Soviet Union and then of China and North Korea. If the big Stalinist states they love to hate are today's incarnation of the Catholic Church, then the Sparts are bit like modern-day Jesuits, but of the bad and stupid kind. They are willing to defend the indefensible in twisted dialectical moves that would defeat the imagination of modern-day theologians, exporting a weird version of US-American colonial Marxism. They act as the shock troops of their own version of the Vatican to spread the gospel, while bizarrely supporting oppressive states in order, they claim, to defend workers rights.

A quick glance at their newspaper *Workers Hammer* and the folded over pages of *Workers Vanguard* they like to carry around to tempt readers with exposés of the crimes of their enemies quickly reveals that their main enemies are actually other groups on the left. They target these rival groups as what they call 'OROs' ('Ostensibly Revolutionary Organisations') which they aim to destroy and then pick over the remains to feed their own organisation. Their papers were actually the best source of information on rival revolutionary groups for many years (a gap in the market that was then filled by the Communist Party of Great Britain – Provisional Central Committee's dirtsheet *Weekly Worker*). The groups on the left they most like to bait and break up are sections of rival internationals to their own International Communist League (Fourth Internationalist). For many years, the tagline of their forerunner organisation, 'The International Spartacist Tendency', was 'Reforge the Fourth International' (a slogan pinched by a member who was expelled and who set up his own international later on).

One notorious foray by the Sparts into the

heart of the beast was during the disastrous Soviet invasion of Afghanistan in 1979 when they recruited a villager in the Birmingham branch of the International Marxist Group (IMG, a forerunner of today's Socialist Resistance and at that time British Section of the Fourth International) and formed the 'Communist Faction' to argue in a not-so-subtly-coded way for their line: Hail Red Army! Their attempts to provoke what they called a 'debate' over the question came to a head when a 1980 meeting of the IMG Central Committee called them on this and the valiant comrades happily admitted it, raising their fists and shouting 'Long Live the International Spartacist Tendency' before marching out the room.

It is partly because the catch-cry 'police agent' has had such a pernicious history in the British far-left (thanks, mainly, to the antics of the Workers Revolutionary Party who went for full-blown conspiracy versions of the accusation to attack other groups) that the left has been reluctant to name the Sparts as such as police agents. How could we know? But the softly-muttered consensus among members of most left organisations over the years that have been subjected to Spart tirades is that it is most probable that, if we look at the damage they have wrought among us, they surely must be financed by CIA.

They are viewed as evangelists for a parody of Marxism configured as a creed to be spread from the United States, and they have often been lucky not to be strung up; their destructive interventions in left meetings are a wonder to behold (once) and then unbearable, driving away anyone coming close to Marxism for the first time. They are much-disliked, and it is understandable, perhaps, that they feel this distrust by the locals in their bones when they venture overseas. All the more so when they have targetted members of OROs by being very friendly, culturally inappropriate in the British left, with rumours that they then encouraged members to undergo psychoanalysis (a rather strange American version of it).

The Sparts defend relics of the True Cross, putting the natives in their place when those natives dare to challenge the civilising influence of Marxist theory; one current favourite doing the rounds is their article reproduced from their South

African outpost called 'Against Black Nationalist Slanders of Marx and Engels'. They want to recruit the locals to build their organisation and spread the word, but they have been caught out more than once complaining at the backward nature of peoples who just don't seem to get the message; in 1997, for example, the then Pope of the Spartacists James Robertson was recorded as referring to Albania, the only Muslim country in Europe, as a nation of goat-fuckers. Robertson would be a good role for Liam Neeson or Andrew Garfield if it wasn't that (unlike those two reactionary turncoats) James kept the faith until he met his maker.

Actually, comparisons between the Jesuits, a canny crew with a sophisticated range of casuistical justifications for allying with the right or, if necessary, with the left, and the Sparts whose speciality is hectoring interventions which persuade nobody, are rather inaccurate. That's what Scorsese's film, if it really is about the Sparts, gets wrong. He should really have depicted his priests not as sophisticated sensitive souls agonising about the cultural differences that lead other people along their own path to salvation, but as all-too-certain raving evangelists screaming at would-be converts to bludgeon them into submission and obedient membership of their own sect.

This little group is actually nothing more than sectlet with a handful of members, and the resources of their base in the USA are getting overstretched as they continue to shrink. They are still good for a few minutes free entertainment on the fringes of a national demonstration, but you don't find the Spartacist League around in Britain much beyond London these days, thank God, and their barking missionaries are usually mercifully reduced to silence.

25

FOURTH INTERNATIONAL IN MANCHESTER GROUP

The 2013 science fiction thriller *Gravity* raises a question as to who is in charge of the plot of a film; the main characters – in this case Lieutenant Matt Kowalski and Dr Ryan Stone – or the actors who play them, George Clooney and Sandra Bullock, or, perhaps more likely still, the director, here Alfonso Cuarón for a film he co-wrote with his son Jonás. Cuarón has good radical form, directing the best of the crop of little boy wizard films with *Harry Potter and the Prisoner of Azkaban* in 2004, and then, two years later, a film he also wrote, *Children of Men* (a film that twisted to the left a 1992 novel by Tory Peer P. D. James). In other words,

Cuarón is really the main man here, taking bad material and making good of it.

It is then too easy to be misled by the antics of Clooney and Bullock. They look like the stars, up among the real stars on the NASA Explorer Space Shuttle to fix the Hubble Space Telescope. But, when they are hit by debris resulting from a Russian missile attack on one of its old pieces of equipment, it looks like Clooney and Bullock will both soon be dead meat. It is Clooney who pegs out first, reappearing in one of Bullock's later hallucinations as she works her way into an abandoned Russian Soyuz craft and then onto a Chinese Shenzou vehicle, just in time to zoom in and break through the upper atmosphere and arrive safe back on earth.

We are up in space circling the planet for most of the film, getting more than a bird's eye view of home, more than enough, too much to work out what is really going on down below. Instead, in a hyper-real internationalist perspective on the world, we navigate in this film the vain attempts by nation states to project themselves into space, into territory they do not yet control. Just as in *Chil-*

dren of Men Cuarón was able to make us see something about our reality that we could not already see, to see more of it, so in Gravity, he was able to show us how little we are, little bit players in our national struggles; we have to step beyond the nation state, beyond earth itself, to get a better perspective on what is really going on.

FIIMG

The Fourth International in Manchester Group (FIIMG) is, let's be honest, one of the smaller, if not the smallest of revolutionary organisations. If it were really led by George Clooney (which is a plausible supposition) then his partner Sandra Bullock would be rolling her eyes wondering what an earth he is doing most of the time tangled up with those old macho leftists who are tangled up in turn with the tangled lines of old clapped out group leaders. She's the one who will survive this. But it's not even down to George, this thing.

Cruciverbalists will detect in the initials FIIMG 'Fourth International', of course, and then 'IMG' which will remind old Trotskyists in Britain of the

International Marxist Group, some of whose ex-members are accumulating a valuable public archive of material in *Splits & Fusions*; that's an invaluable accompaniment to this FIIMG Mapping the English Left through Film project. The current incarnation of the IMG as British Section of the Fourth International is Socialist Resistance, SR, which might lead you to expect FIIMG to praise SR and the FI and attack the rest as pretenders. Not so, because the Fourth International has always comprised a weird mix of old-line Trotskyists, surrealists and libertarians, and all the more so today when it includes members around the world from very different revolutionary traditions; it is a space for action and critical reflection.

Ok, take a deep breath and admit it, there is now more than one 'fourth international', in the sense that there are actually many groupings of revolutionaries who link politics around the globe; you need but two Trotskyists to found a party, three to build an international, and four to produce a split. The Fourth International is so popular, there are many of them. Maybe that is one reason why we, FIIMG, are actually less than one.

We need to acknowledge the others racing around the globe in hyperspace because we are hit by their debris every now and again.

Next down in size after the Fourth International with credible continuity with the organisation founded by Trotsky and his followers in 1938 are, number two, the very nice on the whole comrades of the International Marxist Tendency, whose British section inside the Labour Party is named for its newspaper *Socialist Appeal*. Next down on the list, number three and four in the international hit parade, are two internationals with so few members here as to make them inconsequential to the British scene (unlike the other local groups, LOL), the Fourth International *La Vérité*, followers of Pierre Lambert (of which the British Section is 'FI Britain'), and the Latin-American 'Morenoite' International Workers League, whose British Section is confined pretty much to the Old Swan district of Liverpool (where it is called the International Socialist League). The British SWP runs its own outfit called the International Socialist Tendency, a fifth contender on the world stage.

Sixth, there is a one half of the Committee for

a Workers International (with a very small group in Britain called Socialist Alternative), though internationally the 'majority' and renamed in early 2020 the International Socialist Alternative; and, in seventh place, the other half of the Committee for a Workers International, the 'minority', still staggering on under its original name after a disastrous split in 2019 that was very much to do with London-centric control-freakery by one of its few remaining live groups, the Socialist Party. There are still tinier 'internationals', some of which still claim the title 'Fourth International' (fragment fall-outs from the sexual abuse scandals that spawned the current thankfully much-reduced version of the Workers Revolutionary Party and Socialist Equality Party, and some going where no one has gone before, or will do, to the 'Fifth International' of Workers' Power. Unfortunately, the Cuarta Internacional Posadista, which did try to make contact with flying saucers no longer exists except in name.

It all looks very different from space, no doubt, but we didn't need Alfonso Cuarón to tell us that in space no one can hear you scream. It wasn't him. Comrades have given their lives to the tin-pot dictators that run some of these groups, and that's why internal revolutionary democracy is the absolutely indispensable key to building anything that is worth the time and the energy we have left before the world itself heats up and capitalism kills us all. It is small consolation that people are able to escape every now and again and find a revolutionary space to work together instead of against each other.

You can fill out *Gravity* with any old ideological content, even with advertising, recuperate it, and turn it against the left. And you can do the same with each and every group on the left, drag it back into the orbit of contemporary neoliberal capitalism. In fact, that's what many of the so-called revolutionary groups already offer themselves up to, set themselves up for, and then it is all the worse when they try and build their own 'internationals' in their own image, as simple projections onto a global scale of the way they see things on their home ground. FIIMG escapes that, circling around the British groups, liminal to them, whatever their size, and the various 'internationals' that pretend they are the one.

FIIMG cannot, of course, break free from the Fourth International which was actually founded by Leon Trotsky and fellow anti-Stalinist revolutionaries, not only because the FI can be traced back to the historical origins of revolutionary socialist struggle against both capitalism and Stalinism, but also because this Fourth International is the most honest and open about the need to connect with other revolutionary traditions. This Fourth International does its level best to build something from the fragments, to make another world possible, just as FIIMG shows you where those fragments colliding with each other in Britain come from, all the more effectively for you to make your own commitment to take them some place better.

BIBLIOGRAPHY

Aguirre, C. and Klonsky, M. (n.d.) *As Soon As This Pub Closes...* http://www.whatnextjournal.org.uk/Pages/Sectariana/Pub.html (path-breaking)

Callaghan, J. (1984) *British Trotskyism: Theory and Practice*. Oxford: Blackwell. (useful)

Callaghan, J. (1987) *The Far Left in British Politics*. Oxford: Blackwell. (dated)

Frank, P. and Bensaïd, D. (2010) *The Long March of the Trotskyists Contributions to the History of the Fourth International*. London: Resistance Books. (good)

Gittlitz, A. M. (2020) *I Want to Believe: Posadism, UFOs and Apocalyptic Communism*. London: Pluto. (zippy)

Kelly, J. (2018) *Contemporary Trotskyism: Parties, Sects and Social Movements in Britain*. London and New York: Routledge. (terrible)

Maitan, L. (2019) *Memoirs of a Critical Communist:*

Towards a History of the Fourth International. Dagenham: Merlin Books. (impressive)

Mitchell, A. (2011) *Come the Revolution.* Sydney: NewSouth Publishing. (sad)

Parker, I. (2017) *Revolutionary Keywords for a New Left.* Alresford: Zero Books. (excellent)

Riley, S. (2019) *Winter at the Bookshop: Politics and Poverty St Ann's in the 1960s.* Nottingham: Five Leaves. (nostalgic)

Splits and Fusions (m.d.) *Splits and Fusions,* https://splitsandfusions.wordpress.com/ (indispensable)

Tate, E. (2014) *Revolutionary Activism in the 1950s & 60s. Volume 2. Britain 1965 – 1970.* London: Resistance Books. (interesting)

Thornett, A. (2010) *Militant Years: Car Workers' Struggles in Britain in the 60s and 70s.* London: Resistance Books. (inspiring)

CPSIA information can be obtained
at www.ICGtesting.com
Printed in the USA
BVHW030945170720
583970BV00001B/100